NS | Nick Stellino
COOKING WITH FRIENDS 2

Nick Stellino Cooking with Friends 2

The companion cookbook to the popular television series

CREATIVE DIRECTION AND BOOK DESIGN
Lisa Moore

TITLE DESIGN
Rodney Shelden Fehsenfeld Jr.

PHOTOGRAPHY
Therese Frare

EDITOR
Pat Mallinson

ADDITIONAL PHOTO CREDITS

Photo of Lawrence C. C. Chu
page 226, cover and dust jacket
CREDIT: Lori Eanes, San Francisco

Photo of Gale Gand
page 227, cover and dust jacket
CREDIT: Victor Skrebneski

Photo of Maria Hines
page 227, cover and dust jacket
CREDIT: Amos Morgan

Photo of Andy Husbands
page 228, cover and dust jacket
CREDIT: ©Webb Chappell Photography

Photo of Wade Wiestling
page 229, cover and dust jacket
CREDIT: Nanci Stellino

COPYRIGHT ©2011 Nick Stellino
ALL RIGHTS RESERVED.

ISBN 978-0-974-02864-4

PRINTED IN KOREA

No part of this book may be reproduced in any form or by any electronic or mechanical means, including information storage and retrieval devices or systems, without prior permission from the publisher, except that brief passages may be quoted for review.

NS | Nick Stellino
COOKING WITH FRIENDS 2

PHOTOGRAPHS | Therese Frare

Stellino Productions
SHERMAN OAKS, CALIFORNIA

MASSIMILIANA BOCCATO

I WOULD LIKE TO DEDICATE THIS BOOK TO MY MOTHER, Massimiliana Boccato. At a time when most Italian mothers were glad to have their sons living with them at home well into their late 20s and early 30s, my mother gave me permission to come to America when I was only 17 years old. It was easy for me; it was tremendously painful for her. Her sacrifice gave me the opportunity to become the man I am today.

My brother Mario took this photo of us when she came to visit us in America. She is still this beautiful today... she still cooks better than me... and she always will!

■

Someone's in the kitchen with Nick...

Chef Lawrence C. C. Chu 14
Chef Chu's | Los Altos, California

Chef Sylvain Delpique 36
David Burke Townhouse | New York

Chef Michael Galata 46
Osteria del Circo | New York

Chef Gale Gand 60
TRU | Chicago

Chef Maria Hines 76
Tilth | Seattle

Chef Andy Husbands 90
Tremont 647 & Sister Sorel | Boston

Chef Rick Moonen 104
Rick Moonen's rm seafood | Las Vegas

Chef Brian Poor 124
Portland City Grill | Portland, Oregon

Chef Kent Rathbun 140
Abacus | Dallas ~ Jasper's Restaurants | Texas

Chef Kevin Rathbun 156
Rathbun's, Krog Bar & Kevin Rathbun Steak | Atlanta

Chef John Tesar 174
The Tesar Restaurant Group | Dallas

Chef Wade Wiestling 188
The Oceanaire Seafood Room | Minneapolis

Chef Jason Wilson 208
Crush | Seattle

table of contents

APPETIZERS

Brown-Sugared Pork Belly, Creamed Cabbage & Mustard Greens	164
Gnudi with Arugula Pesto & Tomato 'Spuma'	54
Grilled Honey-Glazed Quail with Watercress Salad	25

SALADS

Arugula, Romaine & Radicchio Salad with Glazed Pine Nuts, Prosciutto Chips & Gorgonzola Dressing	101
Baked-Potato Salad	141
Chef Chu's Famous Chicken Salad	29
Cucumber-Melon Salad with Minted Ricotta	213
Fig & Pepper Cress Salad with Goat's Milk Yogurt, Goat Cheese, & Meyer Lemon & Honey Vinaigrette	179
Grilled Salmon Salad with Grilled Romaine Hearts, with Blue Cheese & Bacon Vinaigrette	198
Ozette Potato Salad	85
Red & Gold Beet Salad	134
Steak & Salad with a Balsamic-Parmesan Dressing	185
Tomatoes & Bread Salad	154

SOUPS

Asparagus Soup with a Confit of Peppers & Asparagus Tips	171
Cauliflower & Parmesan Soup with Cured-Olive Crostini	161
Champagne Oyster Stew	125
Chilled English Pea Soup with Jumbo Lump Crab	105
Kabocha Bisque	18
Rick's New England Clam Chowder	109

PASTA

Andrew's Mac & Cheese	121
Fillet of Tomatoes Pasta	34
Garlic & Oil Pasta	33
Olive Oil-Poached White Anchovies & Squid-Ink Spaghetti, Sicilian Style	175
Pasta with Braised Sausages & Ricotta Parmigiana	86
Spaghetti & Meatballs	57

ENTRÉES

Andy's First Place BBQ Glazed Pork Tenderloin with Bacon-Corn Relish & Cheddar Grits	93
Applewood-Smoked Jalapeño Shrimp	145
Asparagus & Black Trumpet Mushroom Risotto with Truffle Foam	106

Basil-Garlic Braised Manila Clams	135
BLT Burrata with Chipotle-Tomato Dressing	37
Brown Sugar-Brined, Stove Top-Smoked Wild Salmon	132
Butternut Squash Risotto	81
Cajun Roasted Chicken Breasts with Shrimp Jambalaya Hash	143
Chicken Chicharrones with Fresh Oregano	98
Chinese-Style Tea-Steamed Halibut Steaks with Scallions, Ginger & Fermented Black Beans	191
Clams with Sausage & Tomatoes	43
Eggplant Ratatouille with Lemon-Marinated Chicken Breasts	79
Fluke with Potato Gnocchi, Fava Beans & Mustard Sauce	115
Fresh Basil Beef	21
Garlic & Lemon Grilled Shrimp with Warm Potato, Arugula & Chorizo Salad	189
Garlic-Roasted Whole Dungeness Crab & Arugula-Fennel Salad	127
Gung Gung's Home-Style Oxtail Stew	27
Hot Chili Grilled Alaskan Sockeye with Fresh Summer Mango Salsa	193
Lime & Curry-Marinated Grass-Fed Rib-Eye Steaks with Cucumber & Honeydew Melon Chutney & Spiced Basmati Rice	177
Meatball Sandwiches	59
Minnesota-Style Walleye & Wild-Rice Cakes	200
Nick's Chili-Spiced Burgers	122
Nine-Spice Scallops	212
Orange Blossom Ribs	23
Pan-Roasted Wahoo with Eggplant Caviar & Local Tomato-Basil Salad	158
Poached Calamari Ceviche	118
Pork Chops with Zenzero Sauce	221
Pork Ragù	215
Potato-Wrapped Tuna Stuffed with Crab & Cucumber, Served with Pineapple Carpaccio & Ponzu Dressing	39
Salmon with Vodka & Lemon Sauce	205
Salt-Crusted Branzino	48
Slow-Braised Short Ribs with Parsley Pistou	218
Smoked Bacon-Wrapped Rabbit Loin with Wilted Spinach & Grapefruit Jus	41
Stove-Top Braised Octopus	209
Tortino of Artichokes & Calamari	47
Veal Milanese with Tomato Pesto, Salad & Shaved Parmesan	137
Veal Scaloppine alla Romana	53

SIDES

Cauliflower Tabouleh	210
Fat Choy Purses	15
Fried Capers	207
Limed Sour Cream	99
Pan-Fried Potatoes with Peppers & Shallots	44
Radicchio & Spinach Sauté with Lemon Zest & Garlic	207
Roasted Asparagus with Parmesan Cheese	223
Salsa 101	99
Tomato Sauce	89
Yams with Meringue	77
YaYa's Eggplant Fries with Confectioners Sugar	157

BREAKFAST & BRUNCH

Bacon & Eggs with Niman Ranch Bacon & Duck Eggs	148
Cheesy Scrambled Eggs in Ham Cups	70
Eggnog French Toast with Blueberries & Brown Sugar-Crusted Bacon	61
Flavored Coffees	65
Sea Scallop Benedict with Country Ham Grits & Tabasco Hollandaise	166
Vita's Ricotta Doughnuts	63

DESSERTS

Almond Pound Cake with Strawberries & Mascarpone Cream	110
Banana Cream Pie Spoons	72
Cannoli	49
Chocolate-Dipped Cake Lollipops	71
Chocolate Meringue Tart	152
Dried Cherry-Chocolate Fudge Cookies	151
Easy Chocolate Mousse	187
Gooey Toffee Cakes with Toasted-Pecan Ice Cream	168
Lemon-Lime Bars	95
Plums Two Ways with Pound Cake	84
Rhubarb Parfait	182
Sticky Toffee Pudding with Butterscotch Sauce & Sour Cream Ice Cream	66
Strawberry Sauce	75
Tiramisù	74
Ultimate Chocolate Chip Cookie, The	91
Warm Banana-White Chocolate Crisp with Macadamia Nut Crumble	203

foreword

It was the spring of 2000, and I had just sat down to relax for a few minutes prior to the evening rush at my Dallas restaurant, Abacus, when I saw, for the first time, Nick Stellino on television. I remember thinking to myself how passionate and articulate he was while demonstrating a recipe, and I immediately respected him as a chef.

I arrived at Abacus later that evening and was in the kitchen talking about how great this guy Nick Stellino was when all of a sudden a hostess came back and said that I had a call. Believe it or not, it was Nick Stellino calling me at my restaurant just hours after I had seen him on TV! He happened to be in town and was planning to visit Abacus. I was shocked and couldn't believe that the voice I was hearing on the other end of the line was the exact same voice I had been intrigued with just hours before. Funny how life works sometimes.

I had the pleasure of meeting Nick when he came into the restaurant. Since then, he has become much more than the person who fascinated me on TV. He has become a true friend whom I admire and look up to in so many areas of my life.

Nick is an exceptional chef, and having cooked with him on several occasions, I know for a fact that you will be able to create incredible memories with the recipes featured in this book. I am honored to have been asked to write this foreword and wish Nick continued happiness and success.

Congratulations, Nick, my friend!

— Kent Rathbun

a note from the chef...

AT THE AGE OF 17, a time when most young men are happy to just stay home and hang out with their friends, I fulfilled my lifelong dream of coming to America. It was about 35 years ago that I arrived in the United States, full of ambitions and hope.

As I learned, life has a funny way of teaching us lessons; most times the message is delivered with unceremonious bluntness and a harsh dose of reality. Even for a born optimist like me, there were many times, following some of my most harrowing failures, when I started to doubt the fulfillment of my dreams.

During the first few years of my American adventure, I missed my family terribly. I was alone in a foreign land and spoke broken English—and there were only so many hamburgers that I could eat before I started to miss my mother's cooking.

That's exactly how it happened: In an attempt to recreate my own family dishes—those incredible culinary masterpieces that were the cornerstone of every happy moment of my life—I accidentally stumbled onto a new career path. It was not until I connected with my own passion for cooking, however, that I took a chance on myself and—against all odds, and to my great surprise—found myself on the path that got me here today.

Life might not have gone exactly the way I had planned it, but in the end, I got far more than I had ever dreamed of, even if I did not recognize it while it was happening to me.

I think of cooking as a storytelling process in which each ingredient is like a character in my story. When I cook, I think of my family and the stories we used to share around our dinner table, in our family kitchen.

In this book, I wanted to share with all my readers a set of different stories from some of my favorite culinary friends. In the process, I discovered a whole new universe of great recipes and an immense number of new pairings, techniques and flavors.

It turns out that the most beautiful stories are not always the ones we know, but the ones we discover along the way. At the age of 52, working on this project, I felt as if I'd been transformed into a youngster who is experiencing a world of wonderments and great food for the very first time. That's what my latest book and television series have been for me: the adventure of a lifetime. I wanted everyone to tell their story through their food, their own way—and what came out was far more beautiful than I had anticipated.

Some men get lucky, sometimes, in life; some men know it, and some men don't. With this volume of *Nick Stellino Cooking with Friends*, I got very, very lucky, and the best part was that I knew it, too!

I hope you will enjoy this book; it is me at my happiest!

Chef Stellino UNSCRIPTED

WHY DO YOU DO WHAT YOU DO?
Because when I do it, I feel truly happy inside; I feel connected to my place in the world.

WHAT IS YOUR FIRST FOOD MEMORY?
My family making meatballs and tomato sauce using my grandmother's "conserva di pomodoro," bottled crushed tomatoes, packed with basil and olive oil, from her small farm in Sicily.

WHAT IS YOUR FAVORITE DISH TO EAT? TO PREPARE?
Pasta with tomato sauce…and a few meatballs.

IS THERE A FOOD YOU HATE/DON'T LIKE?
Fried calf brain, or brain of any sort.

IF YOU COULD HAVE ONLY ONE FOOD FOR THE REST OF YOUR LIFE, WHAT WOULD THAT FOOD BE?
Pasta and bread—with meatballs and tomato sauce, of course!

WHAT OR WHO INSPIRES YOU?
My father, Vincenzo, my first life coach, who instilled in me the values that made me the man I am today, was a huge source of inspiration. He fostered in me a desire to make a positive difference through all that I do, and the ambition to deploy my vision and turn it into reality. My father's encouragement and support inspired me to become a storyteller who communicates through the sensuality and captivating flavors of food. To me, that is sheer joy—the kind of joy that I seek to instill in the hearts of the people who connect with my passion. Thanks in so many ways to my father, I know who I am and what I can do. Now, I just want to do it—life is short! When I come to the end of mine, I know that my last thoughts will not be about the size of my bank account, but about the special moments of the life I have lived and about the people I have loved, sitting around my dinner table laughing, talking and eating my food. They're my inspiration.

Chef Lawrence C. C. Chu
Chef Chu's | Los Altos, California

Fat Choy Purses
Kabocha Bisque
Fresh Basil Beef
Orange Blossom Ribs
Grilled Honey-Glazed Quail with Watercress Salad
Gung Gung's Home-Style Oxtail Stew
Chef Chu's Famous Chicken Salad

NS
Garlic & Oil Pasta
Fillet of Tomatoes Pasta

Fat Choy Purses

LAWRENCE C. C. CHU

Makes 8 purses

These auspicious Fat Choy Purses are often served during Chinese New Year as a symbol of prosperity and wealth. Fat choy is also the name for black hair moss in Chinese, which lends its symbolic meaning to the garnish.

COOKING TIME: 30 to 40 minutes

FOR THE FILLING:
1 2-inch piece carrot, diced into ¼-inch cubes
32 peas
¼ pound bay scallops
¼ pound medium-sized prawns, each cut into 6 to 8 pieces
1 tablespoon Pompeian® Extra Light Tasting Olive Oil, for stir-frying the filling
1 thumb-size ginger slice, minced
1 green onion, white part only, minced
¼ pound cooked Dungeness crabmeat, moisture squeezed out
4 fresh black mushrooms, diced
4 water chestnuts, diced
1 tablespoon chicken broth
¼ teaspoon salt
¼ teaspoon white pepper
1 tablespoon cornstarch paste

FOR THE WRAPPERS:
8 egg whites
1½ teaspoons cornstarch paste
Pompeian® Extra Light Tasting Olive Oil, for pan-frying the wrappers

FOR THE GARNISH:
8 cooked carrot cubes
8 to 10 green-onion tops (green part)
2 tablespoons dried black hair moss (*fat choy*)

1 recipe Kabocha Bisque (Optional; see recipe on page 18.)

TO PREPARE THE FILLING:
Begin by water-blanching the first 4 filling ingredients. Heat 1½ quarts water to a boil in a saucepan. Add the carrot cubes and blanch 1½ minutes until soft. Add the peas and blanch 30 seconds. Remove with a strainer, and drain. Add the bay scallops and prawns to the water; blanch 1 minute. Remove and drain. Set aside 8 of the blanched carrot cubes for the garnish.

Next, blanch the garnish ingredients. Blanch the green-onion tops (which will be used for ties for the purses) for a few seconds just until they become flexible. Transfer to a cutting board. Slit the thick onion tops in half lengthwise to make tying easier. Dip the black hair moss in hot water for a few seconds to soften. Set aside on a garnish plate with the reserved carrot cubes and the green-onion tops.

Finish by stir-frying the filling ingredients: Heat 1 tablespoon oil in a wok over medium-high heat. Add the ginger and minced green onion, and stir-fry a few seconds. Add the blanched filling ingredients and the crabmeat, mushrooms and water chestnuts, and stir-fry for 1 minute. Add the chicken broth, salt and pepper, and stir-fry 1 minute. Add 1 tablespoon cornstarch paste and stir well. Transfer the filling to another plate to cool.

TO PREPARE THE WRAPPERS:
Place the egg whites and 1½ teaspoons cornstarch paste in a bowl. Beat lightly until the egg whites become smooth but remain clear. Use a paper towel to remove any air bubbles on the surface.

Heat an 8-inch frying pan over medium heat. Wipe on a light coating of oil with a paper towel. Add about 3 tablespoons egg white batter to the pan, tilting the pan to cover the bottom with a thin coating; dab on a little extra batter to repair any holes.

Fry each wrapper about 1 minute on one side until it turns opaque. Gently flip the wrapper over and cook the other side for 30 seconds until set. Oil the pan before frying each wrapper.

Transfer the wrappers to a tray in a single layer to cool. Do not pile wrappers on top of each other, or they may stick together and break.

TO ASSEMBLE:
Spoon 2 tablespoons of filling into the center of each wrapper. Gather up the edges to enclose the filling. Wrap a green-onion tie twice around the "neck" of the purse and tie into a knot. Trim off uneven edges above the tie with scissors, leaving a half inch above. Set the purses aside on a plate.

The purses can be made hours ahead, covered, and refrigerated. To reheat, place the purses on a plate on a steamer rack. Cover, and steam over boiling water for 1 to 2 minutes. Remove to garnish. To garnish, lightly mash the reserved carrot cubes and place on top of each purse. Place a few strands of black hair moss over the carrot.

TO SERVE:
The Fat Choy Purses may be served over sautéed greens such as pea shoots or spinach leaves, or may be served with Kabocha Bisque. (See recipe on page 18.) To serve with the bisque, ladle the soup into wide soup bowls and place a purse in the center of each serving.

CHEF STELLINO'S SUGGESTED WINE PAIRING: *Terras Gauda* Abadía de San Campio Albariño

Chef Chu UNSCRIPTED

WHY DO YOU DO WHAT YOU DO?

I enjoy talking and eating, so having a restaurant suits my personality perfectly.

WHAT IS YOUR FIRST FOOD MEMORY?

My earliest food memories came about at an early age when my mother took me shopping with her in the open-air markets in China and Taiwan. When I was old enough, I carried her grocery bag and looked forward to seeing all the different kinds of foods prepared and sold in the marketplace.

WHAT IS YOUR FAVORITE DISH TO EAT? TO PREPARE?

Believe it or not, it is potstickers. It is comfort food to me, and no matter where I go or travel in the world, I can always prepare it from scratch, if flour is on hand. And, of course, you can stuff it with any kind of filling you like.

IS THERE A FOOD YOU HATE/DON'T LIKE?

That's hard to say, because I admit that I enjoy a wide range of food. I can say that I tend not to go for bleu or Roquefort cheeses.

IF YOU COULD HAVE ONLY ONE FOOD FOR THE REST OF YOUR LIFE, WHAT WOULD THAT FOOD BE?

If I had a choice of just one kind of food, it would be rice. I was raised on it and would be happy to eat it until I die.

WHAT OR WHO INSPIRES YOU?

It would definitely be my parents. They were both well educated and traveled widely. They taught me family values at home, proper table manners, and how to eat and enjoy good food.

Kabocha Bisque

LAWRENCE C. C. CHU

Makes 6 to 8 servings

This bisque is made with creamy soy milk, so it has the advantage of being lactose-free. I enjoy serving this soup with a bit of texture, which makes it more interesting to eat.

COOKING TIME: About 40 minutes

1½ pounds kabocha squash, peeled (see Chef's Tips) and seeds removed, cut into 1-inch cubes
2 tablespoons butter or butter substitute
½ medium onion, finely diced
1 thumb-size piece unpeeled ginger, cut in half lengthwise, lightly crushed
4 cups chicken or vegetable broth
1 teaspoon sea salt, or to taste
2 pinches white pepper, or to taste
½ cup plain soy milk

1 recipe Fat Choy Purses (Optional; see recipe on page 15.)

Place the kabocha squash directly on a steamer rack, cover, and steam over boiling water for approximately 20 minutes, until soft. (A fork or chopstick should pierce through easily.) Transfer the squash to a bowl and set aside.

Heat the butter in a soup pot or saucepan. Add the onion and ginger, and stir 1 minute until the onion becomes translucent. Add the broth and squash, and bring to a boil. Simmer briskly for 12 minutes, stirring occasionally. Adjust the seasoning with salt and white pepper to taste. (If you like the soup with some texture, the squash should retain some chunks.)

Remove and discard the ginger. The bisque can be pureed at this point (see Chef's Tips) and reheated later.

Stir in the soy milk and simmer the bisque another 5 minutes; stir occasionally.

TO SERVE:
Ladle the bisque into 6 to 8 soup bowls. To serve with Fat Choy Purses (see recipe on page 15), place the bisque in wide soup bowls and add a fat choy purse in the center of each serving.

ALTERNATIVE SERVING SUGGESTIONS:
Serve with crispy seafood sticks: Fill an 8-inch square egg roll wrapper with lobster, crab, shrimp or a combination of all three, seasoned with salt and white pepper. Roll into a long 5- to 6-inch cylinder about ¾ inch in diameter. Seal the edge with flour paste. Deep-fry the rolls until golden. Ladle the soup into bowls. Place 1 seafood roll into each bowl, with only one end partially submerged, just before serving, so the rest of the roll remains crisp.

Serve with seafood: Divide 6 ounces of crabmeat or lobster meat among 6 to 8 soup bowls, and ladle the soup over it. The heat of the soup will warm the seafood. Garnish with a drizzle of soy milk, green-onion slivers and freshly ground black pepper.

CHEF'S TIPS: The easiest way to peel a kabocha squash is to cut it into large pieces. Use a sharp knife to cut away the peel, then cut the squash into smaller chunks and steam as directed.

To make a smoother-textured bisque, process the bisque in batches in a food processor fitted with the blade until finely pureed. Alternatively, puree half of the soup and leave the other half slightly chunky. Combine the two and reheat the bisque.

Add toasted slivered almonds or shelled sunflower seeds to the bisque as an optional garnish.

Fresh Basil Beef

LAWRENCE C. C. CHU

Makes 6 to 8 servings

This dish can be served in a clay pot or heatproof casserole. Fresh basil, garlic and chilies will permeate the air and suffuse the beef with flavor.

COOKING TIME: 10 to 15 minutes

1½ pounds flank steak
2 cups cold water
1 teaspoon unseasoned meat tenderizer

FOR THE MARINADE:
½ teaspoon garlic powder
3 tablespoons soy sauce
2 tablespoons dry sherry
1 egg, beaten
2 tablespoons cornstarch
2 tablespoons Pompeian® Extra Light Tasting Olive Oil

FOR THE SEASONING SAUCE:
¼ cup dry sherry
¼ cup soy sauce
2 tablespoons C&H® or Domino® Sugar, or to taste

½ cup Pompeian® Extra Light Tasting Olive Oil, for pan-searing
2 tablespoons sesame oil, for stir-frying

SPICES:
10 garlic cloves, halved lengthwise
5 fresh red jalapeño chilies, seeds intact (optional; see Chef's Tip), stems removed, halved lengthwise
2 stalks green onion, white part only
10 thumb-size slices of ginger

20 to 25 fresh basil leaves, stems removed
1 teaspoon Shaoxing (rice wine)

SPECIAL EQUIPMENT: 1 medium-sized Chinese clay pot or heatproof covered casserole

Trim the fat and gristle from the steak. Slice the flank steak lengthwise into 1-inch-wide strips. Slice the strips crosswise into 1-inch by 1½-inch chunks. Pound the pieces with the back of a cleaver to flatten and tenderize. Mix cold water with the meat tenderizer in a large bowl. Add the steak, mix well, and set aside in the refrigerator for 30 minutes. Drain well.

After draining, return the steak to the bowl. Combine the steak with the marinade ingredients, adding them in the order listed and mixing well after each addition. Set aside for 20 minutes.

Combine the seasoning sauce ingredients in another bowl. (If using a clay pot, preheat it on low to medium heat over a direct flame or electric burner to prepare it for serving. Keep warm.)

First, pan-sear the meat. Heat ½ cup of oil in a large wok until smoking. Lay half of the steak pieces flat in a single layer in the oil. Pan-sear for 30 seconds without turning, until seared golden brown. Turn once and brown the other side for 30 seconds. Remove the pieces to a plate. Reheat the oil over high heat. Repeat the pan-searing with the remaining beef. Remove all oil from the wok.

Next, stir-fry and braise. Reheat the wok over very high heat. Add the sesame oil. Add the garlic and stir-fry until golden brown and fragrant. Add the remaining spices and stir-fry a few seconds. Return the steak to the wok and toss with the spices for 30 seconds. Add one-third of the seasoning sauce at a time, tossing the steak vigorously for 30 seconds after each addition to reduce the sauce. Add half the basil leaves and toss vigorously over high heat until the sauce reduces by half. The steak should be slightly pink in the middle, and there should be a little sauce on the bottom of the wok, enough to glaze the beef.

To serve in a clay pot, immediately transfer the steak mixture to the preheated clay pot. Top with the remaining basil leaves and sprinkle with rice wine. Cover the pot, then place it on a heatproof platter protected with a folded clean, dry towel. Bring to the table and lift and remove the lid in front of your guests. (Can be served in a heatproof covered casserole preheated in a 300-degree oven for 10 to 12 minutes.)

Alternatively, to serve on a platter, transfer the beef to a warm platter and top with fresh basil leaves. Cover the platter with foil or a lid, and bring to the table. Lift the lid or foil in front of your guests.

The basil should be slightly wilted and fragrant using either serving method.

CHEF'S TIP: To make the dish hot and spicy, leave the seeds in the red jalapeños.

CHEF STELLINO'S SUGGESTED WINE PAIRING: *Elements by Artesa* Cabernet Sauvignon

Orange Blossom Ribs

LAWRENCE C. C. CHU

Makes 8 to 10 servings

This dish is characteristic of eastern Chinese cuisine, which uses soy sauce in a cooking technique called "red cooking." Pork ribs are braised in a piquant sauce flavored with star anise, fermented red bean curd and orange juice. The redness of the sauce comes from the addition of red wine lees.

COOKING TIME: Approximately 2 hours

3 pounds pork spareribs, rinsed
3 quarts water

FOR RED WATER (YIELDS ABOUT 9 CUPS):
9 cups water
5 whole star anise
½ cup red wine lees (also called "red rice"—available at Asian markets and herbalist shops)

2 tablespoons Pompeian® Extra Light Tasting Olive Oil
3 thumb-size slices fresh ginger
3 green onions, cut into 3-inch lengths
2 cubes fermented red bean curd

¼ cup soy sauce
2 tablespoons dry sherry
1 orange, quartered and seeded, or 1 cup orange juice
3 ounces Chinese rock sugar or ¼ cup C&H® or Domino® Sugar, or to taste

Cut the spareribs into individual ribs.

Bring 3 quarts of water to a boil in a 14-inch wok. Add the ribs and simmer briskly for 10 to 15 minutes. Remove the ribs, and drain.

Prepare the Red Water by bringing the 9 cups water, star anise and red wine lees to a simmer in another pot. Simmer for 10 minutes until the red color is released. Remove from the heat, and pick out and reserve the star anise. Strain the Red Water through a fine sieve, reserving the liquid. Discard the red wine lees.

Heat 2 tablespoons oil in a Dutch oven. Add the reserved star anise, and the ginger and 3-inch pieces of green onion; stir-fry a few seconds until fragrant. Add the fermented bean curd and 5 cups of the Red Water. Bring to a boil, stirring to dissolve the cubes of bean curd.

Add the ribs, and stir to coat evenly with the red sauce. Add the soy sauce and sherry. Squeeze the orange quarters over the ribs and add the rinds to the pot. Return to a boil and position the ribs to make sure they are covered with liquid.

Cover the pot and briskly simmer for 30 minutes. Add 1 cup of the remaining Red Water about every 30 minutes to keep the ribs covered with liquid. After 1 hour, or halfway through the braising process, add the sugar and stir until it is dissolved. (See Chef's Tips.) Continue to simmer briskly for another 45 minutes to 1 hour, for a total cooking time of about 2 hours. Watch the ribs carefully to prevent burning; stir occasionally to reposition the ribs, and reduce the heat if necessary.

During the last 30 minutes of cooking, remove the lid to allow the sauce to reduce to a syrupy consistency with only a little sauce left on the bottom of the pot to glaze the ribs. The rib meat should be fork-tender, soft and succulent, but still remain on the bones.

TO SERVE:
Stack or arrange the ribs neatly in a warm Chinese sandy clay pot or wide serving bowl.

CHEF'S TIPS: This dish is better the second time around. You can prepare the ribs a day or two ahead, cover, and refrigerate. Add a little water, if the ribs appear dry, before reheating in the microwave.

The sugar is added halfway through the braising stage because sugar tends to make meat seize up and toughen when added too early.

**CHEF STELLINO'S
SUGGESTED WINE PAIRING:** *Bodega Septima* Malbec

Grilled Honey-Glazed Quail with Watercress Salad

LAWRENCE C. C. CHU

Serves 8

We serve this quail as an elegant appetizer at banquets. It looks beautiful presented over a fresh green watercress salad tossed with a light lime dressing. You'll love the flavors!

COOKING TIME: Approximately 6 minutes under the broiler or 6 to 8 minutes on a barbecue grill; the quail should not be overcooked.

8 fresh quail (or semi-boneless quail—see Chef's Tips), **halved lengthwise**

FOR THE MARINADE:
¼ cup oyster sauce
¼ cup honey
¼ cup Pompeian® Extra Light Tasting Olive Oil
1 tablespoon C&H® or Domino® Sugar
1 teaspoon salt
½ teaspoon black pepper
6 garlic cloves, minced
12 sprigs Chinese parsley (cilantro)

FOR THE LIME DRESSING:
2 tablespoons white vinegar or Pompeian® Pomegranate Infused White Balsamic Vinegar
2 tablespoons water
2 tablespoons fish sauce
2 tablespoons Kikkoman® Thai Style Chili Sauce
2 teaspoons lime juice (¼ lime)
2 teaspoons C&H® or Domino® Sugar
2 garlic cloves, finely minced
½ fresh red jalapeño chile, seeded, very finely minced

FOR THE WATERCRESS SALAD:
1 bunch watercress, washed, heavy stems removed, drained well
12 cherry or grape tomatoes

Rinse the quail, drain, and pat dry. Set aside.

TO PREPARE THE MARINADE:
Combine the marinade ingredients in a blender. Process until the garlic and parsley are finely minced. Transfer to a bowl. Set aside half of the marinade for basting. Cover and refrigerate.

Brush each quail piece with (or dip into) the remaining marinade, coating both sides generously. Place the quail on a platter and cover with plastic. Chill 1 hour or overnight.

TO PREPARE THE LIME DRESSING AND WATERCRESS SALAD:
Combine the lime dressing ingredients in a bowl. Place the salad ingredients in another bowl. Cover both separately and refrigerate until needed. (Both can be prepared up to a few hours ahead.)

TO BROIL THE QUAIL:
Line a rimmed baking sheet with aluminum foil. Place a grill rack on top of the foil to hold the quail above the cooking juices and produce grill marks. Place the quail skin side up in a single layer on the grill rack. Brush with some of the reserved marinade. Broil 6 to 7 inches from the broiling element for 3 minutes until browned. Turn the quail skin side down, brush with marinade, and broil another 3 minutes until the quail is browned. The quail should be juicy inside and browned well on both sides. The quail is best served and eaten right after cooking.

TO GRILL THE QUAIL:
On an outdoor barbecue, place the quail on an oiled grill grate set over a medium-hot flame or coals. Grill for 3 to 4 minutes on each side to establish grill marks. Remove each piece from the grill when it is finished cooking, and keep warm. The quail is best served right after grilling.

TO SERVE:
Toss the salad lightly with the lime dressing. Divide the salad among 8 individual serving plates. Place 2 quail halves, skin side up and leaning against each other, over the salad greens.

CHEF'S TIPS: Using semi-boneless quail saves time and work. Because they have less bone structure, they must be skewered to lie flat and to be turned on the grill. They are lovely served as appetizers, placed on a banana leaf-lined platter with the salad served on the side.

CHEF STELLINO'S SUGGESTED WINE PAIRING: *Piccini* Chianti Classico

Gung Gung's Home-Style Oxtail Stew

LAWRENCE C. C. CHU

Makes 6 to 8 servings

Gung Gung, my father-in-law, missed the richly flavored comfort food he grew up eating in China, so we would cook this special dish in his honor. If you enjoy homemade pot roast or stew, this will surely become your favorite, too. The oxtails become soft and succulent after being braised slowly, and the sauce is perfect over rice or noodles.

COOKING TIME: 2½ to 3 hours

3 quarts water
3 pounds beef oxtails
2 tablespoons Pompeian® Extra Light Tasting Olive Oil
3 to 4 large ginger knobs, crushed
2 green onions, cut in half
1 celery stalk, including leaves, cut into 1-inch pieces
¼ medium white or yellow onion, cut into 1-inch pieces
3 whole star anise

FOR THE SAUCE:
10 cups water
1 cup ketchup
¼ cup soy sauce
1 to 3 tablespoons chili paste, to taste

1 tablespoon Pompeian® Extra Light Tasting Olive Oil
16 pearl onions, top and root ends lightly trimmed, light outer skin peeled
16 peeled baby carrots
Cornstarch paste as needed for thickening the sauce
16 cherry tomatoes

Heat 3 quarts of water to a boil in a large pot or wok. Add the oxtails, and parboil 15 minutes. Remove the oxtails, and drain. Discard the water.

Heat 2 tablespoons oil in a Dutch oven. Add the ginger, green onion and celery. Stir-fry for 1 minute. Add the white or yellow onion and star anise; stir-fry until the onion becomes translucent.

Add 6 of the 10 cups of water and the remaining sauce ingredients to the stir-fried vegetables; bring to a boil. Add the oxtails, and return to a boil. The liquid should cover the oxtails. If not, add a little water.

Cover and briskly simmer for 30 minutes. Add 1 cup of water about every 30 minutes and stir occasionally to keep the meat submerged so it becomes succulent. Simmer for 2¼ to 2½ hours. Check the oxtails to see if they are almost tender: The meat should be easily penetrated with a fork or chopstick, but remain on the bone.

While the oxtails are braising, heat 1 tablespoon oil in a small frying pan. Add the pearl onions. Pan-fry until the outside becomes lightly browned on the top and bottom. (This helps the onions maintain their shape.) Add the carrots and stir for 1 minute. Add the onions and carrots to the oxtails and bring to a boil. Simmer uncovered for about 30 minutes until the onions and carrots are tender and the sauce becomes slightly reduced.

To thicken the sauce, stir in enough cornstarch paste to make a medium-consistency sauce. Add the cherry tomatoes and simmer for 2 or 3 minutes. They should remain intact and not burst.

Total cooking time should be around 3 hours, or until the meat becomes fork-tender, silken and succulent.

TO SERVE:
Transfer the stew to a large heatproof serving bowl, clay pot or casserole. Serve with steamed rice, cooked pasta or crusty bread.

CHEF'S TIPS: Oxtails are economical and full of flavor. You will be rewarded with a succulent stew if you don't rush the cooking process and if you test the meat for tenderness as it cooks.

This stew is tastier the second day. After cooking, cover and refrigerate. Remove the fat and add a little water if needed before reheating. Make sure the oxtails are thoroughly heated before serving.

CHEF STELLINO'S SUGGESTED WINE PAIRING: *Two Oceans* Cabernet Sauvignon

Chef Chu's Famous Chicken Salad

LAWRENCE C. C. CHU

Makes 12 servings

Our Famous Chicken Salad is quick, healthy, simple and delicious. To maintain the salad's light, fluffy quality, we toss it at the last minute so everything stays nice and crisp. Our light mustard-and-sesame-oil sauce, along with a dash of Five-Spice Salt (see accompanying recipe), gives it a bit of a bite! Some of our customers enjoy sprinkling a little of Chef Chu's Garlic Dipping Sauce (see accompanying recipe) over each individual serving for a different flavor sensation.

COOKING TIME: 25 to 30 minutes

1 pound cooked chicken (about 2 cups)

2 cups Pompeian® Extra Light Tasting Olive Oil
2 ounces rice sticks, pulled apart into smaller pieces

FOR HOT MUSTARD PASTE:
2 teaspoons Colman's hot mustard powder
2 teaspoons water
1 tablespoon sesame oil

Half-head iceberg lettuce, shredded ¼ inch
½ cup julienned carrots
10 to 12 Chinese parsley (cilantro) sprigs with stems, coarsely chopped
½ teaspoon Chinese Five-Spice Salt (See accompanying recipe.)
¼ cup crushed roasted peanuts
1 tablespoon toasted sesame seeds
4 Chinese parsley (cilantro) sprigs, for garnish

FOR FIVE-SPICE SALT:
2 tablespoons salt
¼ teaspoon five-spice powder

FOR CHEF CHU'S GARLIC DIPPING SAUCE (OPTIONAL):
1 cup chicken broth (fat removed)
½ cup soy sauce
6 tablespoons C&H® or Domino® Sugar, or to taste
2 tablespoons minced fresh garlic
¼ cup white vinegar or Pompeian® Pomegranate Infused White Balsamic Vinegar

Hand-shred the chicken meat by pulling it apart in strands along the grain, or julienne it with a knife. Set aside.

To deep-fry the rice sticks, heat the oil in a wok to 375 degrees. Add the rice sticks in small batches; deep-fry each batch a few seconds until puffy but still white. (Do not brown.) Remove, and drain on paper towels.

To make the hot mustard paste, stir the mustard powder and water together in a small bowl to make a paste. Stir in the sesame oil until the paste becomes smooth and shiny.

TO PREPARE FIVE-SPICE SALT:
Combine the salt and five-spice powder in a small skillet. Place over moderate heat, shaking the pan to agitate the ingredients, for about 1 minute.

TO PREPARE CHEF CHU'S GARLIC DIPPING SAUCE:
Simmer the first 4 ingredients in a pan over low heat, stirring until the sugar is dissolved. Remove from the heat; stir in the vinegar. Let stand for 30 minutes. Serve the sauce warm or at room temperature. It will keep for 1 week, tightly covered in the refrigerator.

TO ASSEMBLE:
The secret to the success of this salad is how it is assembled. Place the lettuce, carrot and chopped Chinese parsley in a large salad bowl. Sprinkle Five-Spice Salt evenly over the lettuce mixture. (See Chef's Tips.) Toss well to distribute the salt evenly. Rub the hot mustard paste around the lower sides of the bowl. Add the chicken, peanuts and sesame seeds evenly over the lettuce, reserving some of the peanuts and sesame seeds for garnish. Toss well to distribute the hot mustard paste evenly throughout the salad. Adjust to taste. Add three-quarters of the rice sticks last; toss lightly to distribute evenly. Garnish with the 4 sprigs of Chinese parsley. Reserve the remaining rice sticks to garnish the individual servings.

To serve, mound the salad on individual salad plates. Sprinkle the remaining rice sticks over the top. Sprinkle a few crushed peanuts and sesame seeds on top, and add a few sprinkles of Chef Chu's Garlic Dipping Sauce if you like.

CHEF'S TIPS: You may use leftover cooked chicken (fried, barbecued, rotisserie, steamed, smoked or pan-fried), or duck for a different flavor. Slightly warm the chicken or duck, or serve at room temperature, for richer flavor.

Add the crisp poultry skin, julienned, to add texture and flavor to the salad.

Five-Spice Salt is added to the lettuce first to help it distribute evenly. If added when the mustard paste is tossed in, it can stick to the mustard and have an unpleasant taste. Also, if added too early, it can wilt the lettuce.

**CHEF STELLINO'S
SUGGESTED WINE PAIRING:** *Elements by Artesa* Chardonnay

Garlic & Oil Pasta
Pasta Aglio, Olio e Peperoncino

NICK STELLINO

Serves 4 to 6

3 quarts water, for cooking the pasta (salt optional)
½ cup Pompeian® Extra Virgin Olive Oil
10 average-size garlic cloves, sliced
¼ teaspoon salt, plus more for the cooking water, if desired
¼ teaspoon red pepper flakes
3 tablespoons chopped fresh parsley, divided
1 pound DaVinci® spaghetti or thin spaghetti
5 tablespoons Italian-style bread crumbs, toasted (See Chef's Tip.)
3 tablespoons grated Romano cheese

In a large stockpot, bring the water, with or without the optional salt, to a boil.

Pour the oil into a large sauté pan set on medium heat and cook the garlic until it starts to sizzle, about 3 minutes. Be careful not to let it turn brown and burn. Remove from the heat and add ¼ teaspoon salt, the red pepper flakes and half the parsley.

Add the pasta to the boiling water and cook according to the package directions until it's tender. Drain the pasta well and add it to the large sauté pan with the garlic and oil. Add the remaining parsley and cook over medium heat, stirring well to coat the pasta with the sauce, about 3 minutes. Add the toasted bread crumbs and toss with the pasta until evenly coated. Turn off the heat, add the Romano cheese, and toss to distribute the ingredients.

CHEF'S TIP: To make toasted bread crumbs, heat a nonstick pan over high heat for 2 minutes. Add the bread crumbs, reduce the heat to low, and stir well for 1 to 2 minutes, until the bread crumbs start to brown. Pour the bread crumbs onto a plate to cool off until ready to use.

CHEF STELLINO'S SUGGESTED WINE PAIRING: *Artesa* Estate Reserve Chardonnay

Fillet of Tomatoes Pasta
Pasta al Filetto di Pomodori

NICK STELLINO

Serves 4 to 6

3 quarts water, for cooking the pasta (salt optional)
1 28-ounce can peeled Italian tomatoes (See Chef's Tip.)
4 tablespoons Pompeian® Extra Virgin Olive Oil
5 garlic cloves, sliced
⅛ teaspoon red pepper flakes
¼ teaspoon salt, plus additional to taste
¼ teaspoon black pepper
⅛ teaspoon dried oregano
10 leaves fresh basil, chopped, or 1 teaspoon dried
1 pound DaVinci® spaghetti
3 tablespoons grated Romano cheese

In a large stockpot, bring the water, with or without the optional salt, to a boil.

Strain the tomatoes, reserving the juice separately. Break the tomatoes into small pieces.

Pour the oil into a large sauté pan set on medium-high heat and cook the garlic and red pepper flakes for 3 minutes. Add the tomato pieces, shaking the pan gently to reduce the oil splatter, and cook for 3 minutes. Add the salt, black pepper, oregano and basil, and cook, stirring occasionally, for 2 minutes. Add the reserved tomato juice, bring to a boil, and simmer for 5 minutes. Add salt to taste.

Cook the pasta according to the package directions until just tender. Drain the pasta well and return it to the pot.

Add the sauce to the pasta, stirring continuously to ensure even coating, and cook for 3 to 5 minutes over medium heat. Turn off the heat, add the cheese, and toss until it's distributed evenly.

CHEF'S TIP: I think Italian canned tomatoes are far superior to anything else on the market. They're usually picked and canned when they're ripe and at the peak of flavor. The result is much sweeter than that produced by their American counterparts. Look for them in an Italian delicatessen.

**CHEF STELLINO'S
SUGGESTED WINE PAIRING:** *Elements by Artesa* Merlot

Chef Sylvain Delpique
David Burke Townhouse | New York

BLT Burrata with Chipotle-Tomato Dressing

Potato-Wrapped Tuna Stuffed with Crab & Cucumber, Served with Pineapple Carpaccio & Ponzu Dressing

Smoked Bacon-Wrapped Rabbit Loin with Wilted Spinach & Grapefruit Jus

NS
Clams with Sausage & Tomatoes

Pan-Fried Potatoes with Peppers & Shallots

BLT Burrata with Chipotle-Tomato Dressing

SYLVAIN DELPIQUE

Makes 4 servings

4 8-inch spinach tortillas
8 leaves hydroponic Boston lettuce
4 slices red beefsteak tomato
12 strips crispy bacon
2 8-ounce pieces burrata, cut in half
4 bamboo skewers

FOR THE CHIPOTLE-TOMATO DRESSING:
1 tablespoon chipotle pepper (Canned is fine.)
1 8-ounce can tomato juice
1 tablespoon lemon juice
3 tablespoons Pompeian® Extra Virgin Olive Oil
Salt and pepper

In a medium bowl, whisk together the ingredients for the dressing.

Preheat the oven to 350 degrees.

Place the spinach tortillas on a baking sheet. In the middle of each tortilla, stack 2 lettuce leaves, 1 tomato slice, 3 strips of bacon and 1 piece of burrata. Top with chipotle-tomato dressing.

Fold 2 sides of each tortilla up around the burrata and hold together with a bamboo skewer. Bake for 6 minutes.

Serve the burrata in the wrap, just like a taco; eat with a knife and fork.

Potato-Wrapped Tuna
Stuffed with Crab & Cucumber, Served with Pineapple Carpaccio & Ponzu Dressing

SYLVAIN DELPIQUE

Makes 4 servings

4 6-ounce blocks of tuna
6 ounces jumbo lump crabmeat
1 cucumber, julienned
1 teaspoon hijiki seaweed
1 large Idaho potato, peeled
1 cup potato flakes
Pompeian® Extra Light Tasting Olive Oil
12 thin slices pineapple

FOR THE PONZU DRESSING:
1 8-ounce can tomato juice
3 tablespoons low-sodium soy sauce
3 tablespoons yuzu juice (Lime juice may be substituted for yuzu juice.)

In a medium bowl, whisk together the ingredients for the dressing.

Butterfly each tuna block. Distribute the crab, cucumber and hijiki seaweed among the 4 blocks of tuna.

Using a mandoline, thinly slice the potato lengthwise and dip the slices in the potato flakes. For each serving, place 4 of the potato slices on a plate next to one another, slightly overlapping, between two pieces of Saran™ wrap. Microwave the potatoes for 45 seconds.

Peel back the top layer of Saran™ wrap and place a tuna block on top of the potatoes. Roll the potatoes up around the tuna.

Place the potato-wrapped tuna block in a skillet with some oil and pan-fry for 1 minute on each side. Slice the block of tuna into 5 slices.

TO SERVE:
For each serving, place 3 slices of pineapple on a plate. Place the slices of tuna on top and drizzle with ponzu dressing.

**CHEF STELLINO'S
SUGGESTED WINE PAIRING:** *Artesa* Estate Reserve Chardonnay

Chef Delpique UNSCRIPTED

WHY DO YOU DO WHAT YOU DO?
At 15 I had to make a choice, so I chose cooking school because it is full of excitement, and that is what I needed at that time. As my interest grew, I also understood it would be a difficult career; however, the endless opportunities in this business would be too great to pass up.

WHAT IS YOUR FIRST FOOD MEMORY?
My mom used to make hundreds of cans of ratatouille in summer for the winter months, so growing up, I always had to help out.

WHAT IS YOUR FAVORITE DISH TO EAT? TO PREPARE?
Moroccan couscous.

IS THERE A FOOD YOU HATE/DON'T LIKE?
Horse liver steak! My dad used to bring meat home once a week, and it was often horse liver steak; my brother and I were not allowed to leave the table till we were finished. I do not believe I will ever eat it again.

IF YOU COULD HAVE ONLY ONE FOOD FOR THE REST OF YOUR LIFE, WHAT WOULD THAT FOOD BE?
Moroccan couscous.

WHAT OR WHO INSPIRES YOU?
Being a chef in New York City is an inspiration in itself.

Smoked Bacon-Wrapped Rabbit Loin with Wilted Spinach & Grapefruit Jus

SYLVAIN DELPIQUE

Makes 4 servings

2 rabbit saddles
24 slices smoked bacon
4 cups wilted spinach
Salt and pepper to taste

FOR THE GRAPEFRUIT JUS:
2 cups chicken stock
6 ounces grapefruit juice

Remove the backbone from each saddle, and reserve. Cut each saddle into 2 loins. Layer 6 slices of bacon on top of each other, and place 1 rabbit loin on top. Top with ½ cup of spinach, and season with salt and pepper. Reserve the remainder of the spinach for service.

Wrap the bacon tightly around the meat, tying with butcher twine to hold in place.

TO PREPARE THE GRAPEFRUIT JUS:
Roast the reserved saddle bones and place in a sauce pot with the chicken stock and grapefruit juice. Reduce by half.

TO ASSEMBLE THE DISH:
On the stove top over high heat, sear the bacon-wrapped rabbit for approximately 2 minutes on each side until the bacon becomes crispy. Place in a 400-degree oven for 6 minutes.

Cut the twine away from the rabbit, and thinly slice.

Fan the rabbit slices around the remaining wilted spinach and drizzle with grapefruit jus.

CHEF STELLINO'S SUGGESTED WINE PAIRING: *The Spanish Quarter* Chardonnay-Albariño

Clams with Sausage & Tomatoes

NICK STELLINO

Serves 4

4 tablespoons Pompeian® Extra Virgin Olive Oil
½ pound spicy Italian sausage, out of the casing
4 tablespoons shallots, chopped
1 cup fresh tomatoes, peeled and chopped, or cherry tomatoes cut in half
2 tablespoons fresh parsley, chopped
2 tablespoons fresh basil, chopped
3 cloves garlic, chopped
¼ teaspoon red pepper flakes
2 pounds fresh Manila clams
½ cup Artesa Carneros Chardonnay
½ cup chicken stock
2 tablespoons softened butter

Pour the olive oil into a large pot and cook over high heat for about 1 minute until it starts to sizzle.

Add the sausage meat, reduce the heat to medium-high, and cook for 1 to 2 minutes, stirring well and breaking the meat into smaller pieces with the back of your stirring spoon.

Add the shallots and cook 1 more minute, stirring well. Add the tomatoes and cook 1 more minute, stirring well. Add the fresh herbs, garlic and red pepper flakes, and cook, stirring well, for 1 more minute, then add the clams.

Add the wine, bring to a boil over high heat, and cook for 2 minutes. Add the chicken stock, bring to a boil, and cook for 5 minutes until all the clams have opened.

Using a slotted spoon, remove the clams to a stainless-steel bowl and cover to keep warm. Discard any clams that have not opened.

Reduce the sauce left in the pan by a third, cooking over high heat for 2 to 3 more minutes. Turn off the heat and add the softened butter, stirring well until it melts completely into the sauce.

Serve the clams on individual plates and pour the sauce on top of each serving. Serve with Pan-Fried Potatoes with Peppers & Shallots (see recipe on page 44) and plenty of bread on the side.

CHEF STELLINO'S SUGGESTED WINE PAIRING: *Elements by Artesa* Red Wine

Pan-Fried Potatoes with Peppers & Shallots

NICK STELLINO

Serves 4

5 tablespoons Pompeian® Extra Light Tasting Olive Oil
2¾ to 3 pounds potatoes, peeled, trimmed and cut into ½-inch cubes
2 tablespoons shallots, chopped
1 red bell pepper, cut into small dice
1 yellow bell pepper, cut into small dice
1 green bell pepper, cut into small dice
2 tablespoons garlic, chopped
2 tablespoons parsley, chopped
1 tablespoon softened butter

Pour the oil into a large nonstick sauté pan and cook over high heat until it starts to sizzle.

Add the potatoes and cook for 6 to 8 minutes, stirring every 3 minutes until they start to brown. Using a slotted spoon, remove the potatoes to a bowl. Keep only 2 tablespoons of the oil in the pan; discard the rest.

Over medium heat, bring the oil back to a sizzle (about 1 minute). Add the shallots, stir well, and cook for 1 minute. Add the peppers, stir well, and cook for 3 minutes. Add the garlic, stir well, and cook for 1 more minute. Add the potatoes, stir well, and cook for 2 to 3 more minutes.

Turn off the heat, and add the parsley and butter. Stir well until the butter has melted through, and serve.

Chef Michael Galata
Osteria del Circo | New York

Tortino of Artichokes & Calamari
Salt-Crusted Branzino
Cannoli
Veal Scaloppine alla Romana
Gnudi with Arugula Pesto & Tomato 'Spuma'

Spaghetti & Meatballs
Meatball Sandwiches

Tortino of Artichokes & Calamari

MICHAEL GALATA

Serves 2

¾ pound fresh calamari, cleaned and rinsed
4 ounces artichokes, sliced
½ cup all-purpose flour, or as needed for dredging
Salt and pepper as needed
4 ounces Pompeian® Extra Virgin Olive Oil, plus more for the skillet

FOR THE GARNISH:
Radicchio, thinly sliced
Pompeian® Extra Virgin Olive Oil
Lemon juice (optional)
Mâche (also known as lamb's lettuce)
Micro basil
Fresh-cracked black pepper

Cut the squid's body into thin rings approximately ⅛ inch thick. Rinse the rings and tentacles thoroughly in cold water, then blot dry on absorbent toweling.

Combine the calamari, artichokes, flour, salt and pepper in a large bowl, and mix in the oil slowly.

Add a splash of the oil to a skillet and preheat the oil over medium-high heat. Put the calamari mixture into the pan, forming a cake about ½ inch thick. Cook, turning occasionally, until it's golden brown on all sides, about 6 to 8 minutes. Remove the tortino from the oil and drain briefly on absorbent toweling.

TO PREPARE THE GARNISH:
Season the radicchio with the olive oil and the lemon juice (optional). Spread the radicchio on a plate, then place the tortino on top of it and sprinkle with mâche and micro basil. Finish off with fresh-cracked black pepper.

CHEF STELLINO'S SUGGESTED WINE PAIRING: *Voga* Pinot Grigio

Salt-Crusted Branzino

MICHAEL GALATA

Serves 2

2 whole branzino (1½ to 2 pounds total), **gutted, scaled, cleaned and filleted at the fish market** (4 fillets)
3 tablespoons Pompeian® Extra Virgin Olive Oil (more if necessary), **plus additional to serve at the table**
Coarse sea salt, for seasoning the uncooked fillets
1 zucchini, sliced thinly into chips
2 basil leaves
4 leaves romaine lettuce
6 egg whites
2½ cups kosher salt
3 lemons, quartered

Preheat the oven to 425 degrees. Line a large, rimmed baking sheet with parchment paper. Rub the fish liberally with the oil and season with a pinch of sea salt.

Place a fillet skin side down on the parchment paper. Arrange 4 zucchini slices shingle style on top of the fillet and add a leaf of basil. Cover the fish with a second fillet; the second fillet should be skin side up. Place 2 romaine leaves, crisscrossed, on top of the fish. Repeat this process with the remaining 2 fillets.

Whip the egg whites in a mixing bowl, adding the kosher salt slowly until you have achieved the consistency of wet sand. Cover each pair of fillets with a layer of the egg white-and-salt mixture, packing it tightly and forming it into a large oval shape around the fillets. Place the fish in the preheated oven for 12 minutes. Remove from the oven and let rest for 2 minutes.

Using a fork, pop off the crust from one corner of each of the pairs of fillets—it should come off easily in one piece. Discard the crust and the romaine leaves.

The fillets may be served with or without the skin. Serve the fish with the zucchini slices, lemon quarters and other accompaniments of your choice; have extra olive oil at the table.

**CHEF STELLINO'S
SUGGESTED WINE PAIRING:** *Ca'Montini* Pinot Grigio

Cannoli

MICHAEL GALATA

Serves 2 (makes 4 cannoli)

FOR THE CANNOLI SHELLS:
4 ounces all-purpose flour, plus more as needed
1½ ounces C&H® or Domino® Sugar
2½ ounces Vin Santo or Marsala
¼ teaspoon cinnamon
1 tablespoon butter
1 egg yolk
1 teaspoon vanilla extract
Pompeian® Extra Light Tasting Olive Oil, for frying

FOR THE FILLING:
3 ounces fresh ricotta
1 tablespoon candied orange, finely chopped
2 tablespoons C&H® Powdered Sugar or Domino® Confectioners Sugar, plus extra for dusting the cannoli
⅓ cup mini dark chocolate chips

TO PREPARE THE CANNOLI SHELLS:
In a mixing bowl, mix all the ingredients in order; keep mixing until a ball forms. Cut the ball of dough into 4 equal-size pieces. Roll out each piece in flour as needed until it's very thin—about ⅛ inch thick—and cut it into a 4-inch square. Starting at one point of the square, roll the dough around a cannoli form or a ¾–inch-diameter dowel. Press down on the overlapping edges to seal. Fry for approximately 45 seconds in the oil until golden and crispy. Remove from the oil and remove the cannoli form or dowel. Let cool.

TO PREPARE THE FILLING:
Place the ricotta in a strainer over a small bowl and strain the excess liquid for about an hour. Mix all the ingredients until creamy. Spoon the filling into a pastry bag and pipe some into one end of a cannoli shell, filling the shell halfway, then pipe an equal amount into the other end. Repeat with the remaining shells. Dust with powdered/confectioners sugar.

CHEF STELLINO'S SUGGESTED WINE PAIRING: *Umberto Fiore* Moscato d'Asti

Chef Galata UNSCRIPTED

WHY DO YOU DO WHAT YOU DO?

The reason I do what I do is that cooking and food found me. I grew up in my family's Italian restaurant; I worked in the kitchen washing dishes and helping, and watching my father butcher meat and fish and make sauces and other things. Seeing how much they struggled controlling the consistency of the food and dealing with disgruntled cooks and chefs drove me to help my family by learning fast and working in the kitchen—and I did and also found my passion and love for food and the kitchen and the biz. When it was time in high school to decide what you want to do, so to speak, the only thing for me was cooking. Upon graduating high school, I was put in charge of the kitchen at 18, and the rest just happened.

WHAT IS YOUR FIRST FOOD MEMORY?

My earliest memory of food is my father torturing me during dinners by putting pieces of octopus and squid on my plate because I was literally terrified of them—why, I don't know, but it grossed me out...funny. Equally memorable would be the smells of tomato sauce almost always cooking in my mother's kitchen.

WHAT IS YOUR FAVORITE DISH TO EAT? TO PREPARE?

My favorite food to eat is the momo. The momo is a Tibetan dumpling made from tsampa, a toasted, ground barley flour. The filling varies by region; it's usually vegetable. I think part of my love for momos stems from how I discovered them. I was in Dharamsala, the home of the Dalai Lama in the mountains of northern India. My girlfriend and I befriended a young Buddhist monk. One night, he cooked us his favorite Tibetan food. We cooked and ate together like a family. I will never forget that, or momos!

IS THERE A FOOD YOU HATE/DON'T LIKE?

One type of food that I don't enjoy as much as the rest is certain cheeses. Sorry, but due to the fact that as a child I was extremely allergic to dairy, I shunned it, so my palate for cheeses is still developing. I've tasted them all and love to cook and create with them, but I'm not that guy who can just eat a whole wheel of cheese with bread and wine.

IF YOU COULD HAVE ONLY ONE FOOD FOR THE REST OF YOUR LIFE, WHAT WOULD THAT FOOD BE?

Bacon.

WHAT OR WHO INSPIRES YOU?

In life, I have many inspirations. Outside of cooking, my main inspirations have been my father, for his perseverance and persistence and achievements; my mother, for her huge heart and for being able to hold down any situation; and, most recently, my beautiful girlfriend, who has taught me the importance of travel and opened my eyes to the world.

Veal Scaloppine alla Romana

MICHAEL GALATA

Serves 2

4 3-ounce top round veal cutlets
Salt to taste
½ teaspoon pepper
Flour
2 tablespoons Pompeian® Extra Light Tasting Olive Oil

FOR THE SAUCE:
¾ pound crimini mushrooms, sliced in half
1 ounce capers, rinsed
⅔ cup Artesa Carneros Chardonnay
4 ounces chicken broth
4 ounces butter
¾ teaspoon chopped parsley
Salt and pepper to taste
1 lemon, seeded and cut in half

TO PREPARE THE SCALOPPINE:
Place the veal cutlets 5 inches apart between 2 pieces of plastic wrap and pound with a mallet until very thin—about ⅛ inch thick. Remove the plastic wrap, season with salt and pepper, and dust with flour, patting off the excess flour.

Heat a large sauté pan on medium to high heat, and add the oil. Sear the cutlets on one side until the juices start to come out from the meat. Remove the pan from the heat, turn the cutlets to the other side, and cook for 15 seconds, then remove them to a plate and reserve.

TO PREPARE THE SAUCE:
Add the mushrooms and capers to the pan and return it to the heat. Sauté for 30 seconds, then add the Chardonnay and reduce by half. Add the chicken broth, butter, parsley, and salt and pepper to taste. Simmer until the sauce thickens slightly. Remove the pan from the heat and squeeze lemon juice into the sauce to taste.

Return the veal to the pan and reheat it. Arrange 2 veal cutlets on each plate, and top with the sauce.

CHEF STELLINO'S SUGGESTED WINE PAIRING: *Artesa* Estate Reserve Pinot Noir

Gnudi with Arugula Pesto & Tomato 'Spuma'

MICHAEL GALATA

Serves 2 (makes 4 gnudi)

FOR THE GNUDI:
1 cup whole-milk ricotta cheese
2 eggs
2 1-pound boxes coarsely ground semolina
1 teaspoon salt

FOR THE ARUGULA PESTO (YIELDS 1 QUART):
1 pound arugula, freshly picked, washed 3 times
2 garlic cloves
4 ounces raw pine nuts
4 ounces Pompeian® Extra Virgin Olive Oil
Salt and pepper to taste

FOR THE TOMATO 'SPUMA':
1 dozen ripe plum tomatoes
1 pint grape tomatoes
Salt
Cheesecloth

Roasted cherry tomatoes (optional, for garnish)

TO PREPARE THE GNUDI:
In a large bowl, mix the ricotta and eggs. Form the mixture into 4 small, flattened ovals, then dredge in semolina until completely covered.

Let the gnudi rest for 24 hours in the fridge.

Bring a large pot of water to a boil, season with salt, and poach the gnudi slowly for about 4 minutes until warm inside.

TO PREPARE THE ARUGULA PESTO:
Combine the arugula, garlic cloves and pine nuts in a food processor and pulse until coarsely ground. Drizzle in the olive oil and season with salt and pepper.

TO PREPARE THE TOMATO 'SPUMA':

In a blender, puree the tomatoes and season with salt. Line a strainer with a piece of cheesecloth and strain the tomato puree for 24 hours.

Boil the strained tomato liquid for 2 minutes, remove from the heat, and, with a hand blender, froth the liquid.

TO SERVE:

Place 2 tablespoons of arugula pesto in a bowl, add 2 poached gnudi on top, and spoon foam from the tomato liquid over the gnudi.

OPTIONAL: Garnish with roasted cherry tomatoes.

CHEF STELLINO'S SUGGESTED WINE PAIRING: *Piccini* Chianti Superiore

Spaghetti & Meatballs

NICK STELLINO

Serves 6 to 8

FOR THE MEATBALLS:
2 cups stale bread, cubed
1 cup milk
2 tablespoons garlic, finely chopped
¼ cup fresh Italian parsley, chopped
2 eggs
2 cups freshly grated Pecorino Romano cheese
2 tablespoons C&H® or Domino® Sugar
1 teaspoon cinnamon
1 teaspoon nutmeg
½ teaspoon black pepper
1 pound lean ground beef
1 pound ground veal
1 pound ground pork
8 tablespoons Pompeian® Extra Light Tasting Olive Oil

FOR THE MEATBALL GRAVY:
3 cups **Tomato Sauce** (See recipe on page 89.)
¾ cup beef stock
1 teaspoon salt
½ teaspoon black pepper

1 pound DaVinci® pasta—spaghetti, rigatoni or ziti
2 tablespoons fresh Italian parsley, chopped

TO PREPARE THE MEATBALLS:
Place the cubed bread in a stainless-steel bowl and cover with the milk. Let sit for at least 20 minutes, pour off the milk that has accumulated at the bottom of the bowl, and squeeze the bread cubes to get rid of the extra milk. Break up the softened bread into small pieces; they should look like wet oatmeal.

Mix the pieces of bread with all the remaining ingredients except the olive oil, working until the ingredients are completely incorporated. Shape the mixture into oval meatballs, using ⅓ cup of the meat mixture for each ball.

In a large sauté pan set on high heat, heat the olive oil until sizzling, about 2 minutes. Brown the meatballs for 2 to 3 minutes on each side. Don't crowd the meatballs in the pan when browning; you will need to brown them in several batches.

Remove the first batch of meatballs from the pan and drain on a paper towel or brown paper bags. Repeat with the remaining meatballs. Set aside.

TO PREPARE THE MEATBALL GRAVY:

Combine the tomato sauce, beef stock, salt and pepper in a big pot, stirring well, and bring to a simmer over medium-high heat. Add the browned meatballs to the pot and bring the liquid to a boil. Reduce the heat to medium and cook for 30 minutes.

While the gravy is simmering, add the pasta to boiling water and cook until just tender. Drain the pasta well and return it to the pot. Add half the gravy from the meatball pot and toss it with the pasta. Transfer the pasta to a large serving bowl or platter, and top with the meatballs and the remaining gravy. Sprinkle with the chopped parsley, and serve.

CHEF STELLINO'S SUGGESTED WINE PAIRING: *Elements by Artesa* Cabernet Sauvignon

Meatball Sandwiches

NICK STELLINO

Yields 4 sandwiches

1 cup shredded provolone
1 cup grated Romano cheese
8 warm meatballs (see recipe on page 57), **cut in half**
4 Italian rolls, split in half
2 cups warm meatball gravy (See recipe on page 57.)

Preheat the broiler.

Mix the provolone and Romano. To make each sandwich, place 2 meatball halves on each half of an Italian roll. Moisten each sandwich half with a tablespoon of meatball gravy.

Divide the cheese mixture among the 4 sandwiches.

Place the meatball sandwiches, open-faced, on a baking tray big enough to hold all 4. Cook under the broiler until the cheese begins to brown.

Divide the remaining meatball gravy into 4 portions. Serve each sandwich with a side of the gravy for dipping, along with lots of paper towels—it will be messy!

**CHEF STELLINO'S
SUGGESTED WINE PAIRING:** *Artesa* Artisan Series Napa Valley Cabernet Sauvignon

Chef Gale Gand
TRU | Chicago

Eggnog French Toast with Blueberries & Brown Sugar-Crusted Bacon
Vita's Ricotta Doughnuts
Flavored Coffees: Cinnamon Coffee & Orange Coffee
Sticky Toffee Pudding with Butterscotch Sauce & Sour Cream Ice Cream
Cheesy Scrambled Eggs in Ham Cups
Chocolate-Dipped Cake Lollipops
Banana Cream Pie Spoons

NS Tiramisù
Strawberry Sauce

Eggnog French Toast
with Blueberries & Brown Sugar-Crusted Bacon

GALE GAND

Makes 4 to 6 servings

FOR THE FRENCH TOAST:
2 eggs
1 pinch salt
2 cups eggnog
8 slices brioche (or bakery challah or another soft yellow bread), ¾ inch thick

FOR THE BERRY SAUCE:
½ cup maple syrup
2 tablespoons water
½ pint blueberries (or 1 cup cranberries)

FOR THE BROWN SUGAR-CRUSTED BACON:
1 pound sliced bacon
¼ cup C&H® Golden Brown Sugar or Domino® Light Brown Sugar

½ cup sour cream, for garnish

TO PREPARE THE FRENCH TOAST:
In a medium bowl, whisk the eggs. Whisk in the salt and eggnog. Pour the mixture into a shallow baking dish. Working in batches if necessary, place the bread in the dish and let it soak a few minutes, then turn it and soak on the other side.

Cook the soaked bread on a grill or buttered griddle until golden brown, then turn it and repeat on the other side. Meanwhile, prepare the blueberry (or cranberry) sauce.

TO PREPARE THE BERRY SAUCE:
In a sauté pan, add the maple syrup and water, and bring to a boil. Add the blueberries (or cranberries), and cook till they start to burst and break down. Pour the cooked mixture into a blender and whiz it to make a sauce, or just mash it with the back of a fork. Keep the sauce warm and pour over the French toast, then top with dollops of sour cream.

Serve the French toast with brown sugar-crusted bacon.

TO PREPARE THE BROWN SUGAR-CRUSTED BACON:
In a frying pan, cook the bacon on medium heat, turning once, till you achieve the desired doneness. Place the bacon on a sheet pan and sprinkle with brown sugar. Bake at 400 degrees till the sugar is caramelized. Serve warm.

Vita's Ricotta Doughnuts

GALE GAND

Makes 30 or more doughnuts; recipe may be cut in half

FOR THE DOUGHNUT BATTER:
6 eggs
½ cup C&H® or Domino® Sugar
1 pound ricotta
2½ cups flour
1 heaping tablespoon baking powder
1 teaspoon pure vanilla extract
1 teaspoon grated lemon rind

Canola oil or Pompeian® Extra Light Tasting Olive Oil, for frying
C&H® Powdered Sugar or Domino® Confectioners Sugar, for sprinkling on the doughnuts

SPECIAL EQUIPMENT:
Small ice-cream scoop
Frying thermometer

FOR THE LEMON CREAM DIPPING SAUCE:
2 eggs
½ cup C&H® or Domino® Sugar
⅓ cup freshly squeezed lemon juice (from 3 to 4 lemons)
Freshly grated zest of ½ lemon
Ice, for an ice bath
2 tablespoons unsalted butter, slightly softened at room temperature
½ cup chilled heavy cream

TO PREPARE THE DOUGHNUTS:
Mix the batter ingredients in order with a wooden spoon, being careful not to overmix. You can place the batter in the refrigerator at this point and keep it there till you're ready to fry, up to 48 hours. You may have to increase the frying time slightly to compensate for the colder batter.

Heat the oil in a large saucepan to 325 degrees. Drop the batter by small ice-cream-scoopfuls or teaspoonfuls into the oil and deep-fry for 3 minutes, turning the doughnuts often till golden brown on each side. Break the first doughnut open to check that it is cooked all the way through.

Drain the doughnuts on paper towels or a brown paper bag and sprinkle heavily with powdered/confectioners sugar, or place them in a resealable bag of powdered/confectioners sugar and shake them well to coat. Serve in a bowl or on a platter with a side of the lemon cream as a dipping sauce.

TO PREPARE THE LEMON CREAM DIPPING SAUCE:
Bring about 2 inches of water to a simmer in a large saucepan. In the bowl of a mixer fitted with a whisk attachment (or using a hand mixer), whip the eggs and sugar together until very light

yellow and fluffy. Mix in the lemon juice and lemon zest. Rest the mixing bowl in the saucepan, with the bowl's base resting above—not in—the simmering water. (Pour out some water if necessary.) Cook, whisking occasionally (you don't need to whisk constantly), until the mixture is thickened and custardy, about 10 minutes.

Meanwhile, half-fill a large bowl with ice and cover with cold water. Remove the bowl with the custard in it from the saucepan and whisk in the butter until melted. Rest the bottom of the bowl in the ice bath and let it cool, folding the mixture occasionally to cool and thicken it.

In the bowl of a mixer fitted with a whisk attachment (or using a hand mixer), whip the cream until stiff. Fold it into the cooled lemon custard. Cover, and refrigerate until ready to serve. (The lemon cream can be kept refrigerated for up to 48 hours before use.)

CHEF STELLINO'S SUGGESTED WINE PAIRING: *Artesa* Artisan Series Orange Muscat

Flavored Coffees

GALE GAND

Cinnamon Coffee

Cinnamon stick
Ground coffee

Place a cinnamon stick in the filter of your coffeepot and then add the ground coffee to be brewed. Brew as you normally do, and the hot water will extract the oils of the cinnamon to flavor the coffee. Use any that's left over to make cinnamon coffee ice cubes for your next cup of iced coffee.

Orange Coffee

Peel of 1 orange
Ground coffee

Place the peel of 1 orange in the filter of your coffeepot and then add the ground coffee to be brewed. Brew as you normally do, and the hot water will extract the oils of the orange rind to flavor the coffee with orange essence.

Sticky Toffee Pudding
with Butterscotch Sauce & Sour Cream Ice Cream

GALE GAND

Serves 8 to 10

British sweets have the most wonderful names, like Crundle Pudding, Gooseberry Fool, Blackberry Crumble, Lardy Cakes and Plum Heavies. Sticky Toffee Pudding is a classic from the Lake District way up in the north of England, where it gets bitterly cold, and the term "sticky" is the highest praise such a pudding can receive. This is a very moist date cake that is baked and then soaked with butterscotch sauce, and finally baked again to caramelize the brown sugar.

The sour cream ice cream is the perfect foil for berries and stone fruits in the spring and summer, or apple and caramel desserts in the fall and winter. I love the tanginess the sour cream adds to what might otherwise be just plain old vanilla ice cream.

FOR THE CAKE:
¾ **pound dates, pitted and roughly chopped** (You can use kitchen scissors to do this.)
2½ **cups water**
2 **teaspoons baking soda**
8 **tablespoons** (1 stick) **cold unsalted butter, cut into pieces**
1⅔ **cups C&H® or Domino® Sugar**
4 **eggs**
2 **teaspoons pure vanilla extract**
3¼ **cups all-purpose flour, sifted**
2 **teaspoons baking powder**

FOR THE SAUCE:
2¼ **cups C&H® Golden Brown Sugar or Domino® Light Brown Sugar**
7 **tablespoons unsalted butter**
1 **cup half-and-half**
1 **teaspoon brandy**
¼ **teaspoon pure vanilla extract**

FOR THE SOUR CREAM ICE CREAM (YIELDS 3½ TO 4 CUPS ICE CREAM, OR 8 SERVINGS):
2 **cups sour cream**
1 **cup half-and-half**
2 **tablespoons fresh-squeezed lemon juice**
1 **cup plus** 2 **tablespoons C&H® or Domino® Sugar**
½ **vanilla bean, scraped, or** ½ **teaspoon pure vanilla extract**

TO PREPARE THE CAKE:

Preheat the oven to 325 degrees and line a 9-by-13-inch baking pan with parchment paper.

Combine the dates and water in a saucepan and bring to a boil. Turn off the heat and gradually stir in the baking soda (it will foam up) and set aside.

Using an electric mixer with a whisk attachment, cream the butter until fluffy. Add the sugar, and cream together until fluffy. Without stopping the mixer, add 2 of the eggs and mix until combined. Add the remaining 2 eggs and mix until combined, then add the vanilla.

In a separate bowl, combine the flour and baking powder. Add about ⅓ of this flour mixture and ⅓ of the dates to the creamed mixture, and mix until combined. Repeat until all the flour mixture and dates are integrated into the batter.

Pour the batter into the prepared baking pan and bake about 40 minutes, or until the cake is firm and set in the center. Let it cool in the pan. When the cake is cool, turn it out of the pan onto a baking sheet and peel off the parchment paper. (The recipe can be made through this step up to 2 days in advance.)

TO PREPARE THE SAUCE:

Combine all the ingredients except the vanilla in a saucepan and bring to a boil. Boil 3 minutes, until thickened. Remove the sauce from the heat and stir in the vanilla.

TO PREPARE THE SOUR CREAM ICE CREAM:

Whisk all the ingredients together and let sit, covered and chilled, for at least 1 hour, or overnight.

Pour the mixture into an ice-cream machine and freeze it according to the manufacturer's directions. Meanwhile, place an empty container in the freezer to later store the ice cream in.

TO FINISH:

When you're ready to finish, bring the cake to room temperature and preheat the oven to 400 degrees.

Pour the sauce evenly over the top of the cake. Bake until the sauce is bubbly and the cake is heated through, about 5 minutes. Cut the cake into squares and serve with sour cream ice cream.

Chef Gand UNSCRIPTED

WHY DO YOU DO WHAT YOU DO?

I always say I didn't pick this profession, it chose me. I love my ingredients and how they react to each other, but I also just love "the dance" of cooking. It feels right to me, makes sense in a way nothing else does, and I get the chemistry and physics of it and find it fascinating. I love the movement it takes to create something in the kitchen. It makes me feel like I am an artist as well as a nurturer and an entertainer, all at the same time. Plus I get to connect with people in a way that's really intimate and personal, creating valued memories with them...plus, I love to eat!

WHAT IS YOUR FIRST FOOD MEMORY?

Well, I used to pretend to cook when I was 5 or so, vigorously stirring together flower buds from my mother's day lilies with some little pods off a neighbor's tree and a bit of water—and voilà! Soup! And then there were the mud meatballs, tossed leaf salad and mud pies we made daily; we were even caught on camera by a *Life* magazine photographer making them. But I'm not sure that's REALLY food, so my early tasting memory is tasting the bliss of the simple combination of butter whipped with powdered sugar to make a simple frosting for cakes. I might have been 5 or 6, and my mother was whipping it together for something. After I discovered it, I actually kept a jar of it way under my bed to sneak a taste after bedtime.

WHAT IS YOUR FAVORITE DISH TO EAT? TO PREPARE?

Probably a fried-egg sandwich on caraway rye toast made by my husband, or just a piece of cold fried chicken.

I love to make meatballs, and lots of them. First for spaghetti that night and then for meatball sandwiches later in the week, then reheated on top of pasta. I love to eat them hot or cold and can even be caught stabbing a cold meatball out of the fridge late at night for a snack, eating it almost like a popsicle. I find the secret to good meatballs is to use half beef and half pork. The pork keeps things tender and moist. All-beef ends up with a slightly grainy texture, and too firm.

I also make a lot of apple pies at home, mostly with and for my kids. I have one daughter, Ella, who could eat apple pie for breakfast, lunch and dinner, and so she does when there is one in the house. And my husband says I'm never happier than after I've been crimping a pie crust. I have my great-grandmother's rolling pin and use it to roll the dough so I feel a little like she is there in the kitchen with me, watching over me as I work the dough, carefully and with love.

IS THERE A FOOD YOU HATE/DON'T LIKE?

I detest fruitcake, did even before I lived in England for three years and had to make it all the time for guests at the country-house hotel where I worked. I suppose it was good at one time, but it turned into such an industrial food, more like a construction supply, with its brick-like shape, than food to feed the soul.

IF YOU COULD HAVE ONLY ONE FOOD FOR THE REST OF YOUR LIFE, WHAT WOULD THAT FOOD BE?

Probably eggs. They are so flexible and magical that I don't think I would tire of them.

WHAT OR WHO INSPIRES YOU?

I get inspired from everywhere: artists, paintings, penny candy, my mother-in-law's cooking, other pastry chefs' work, flowers, foreign countries, my painting teacher Moe Brooker from college, my husband, my children, the grocery store, the farmers market, the autumn leaves...stuff like that.

Cheesy Scrambled Eggs in Ham Cups

GALE GAND

Makes 4 servings

This pretty dish is simple to make but impressive to look at. Lining muffin tins with ham serves two purposes. It makes a container for the eggs, and it adds flavor. You can use any cheese you like depending on whether you want a lot of flavor or just a whisper—it's up to you. This is knife-and-fork food, but when I was testing the recipe, I just used my hands.

2 teaspoons butter for greasing the muffin tin, plus more for frying
4 round slices of ham, sliced ⅛ inch thick
8 eggs
¼ cup milk
Salt and black pepper to taste
½ cup grated Cheddar cheese

Butter 4 compartments of a metal muffin tin well. (I use a standard muffin tin, but if you want a bigger cup, you can use one of the jumbo tins; just make sure you have large enough slices of ham for that size.) Fold the ham slices into quarters, then place 1 in each cup and let go to line it with ham. The ham will blossom and ruffle, which is what you want.

Preheat the oven to 375 degrees.

In a bowl, whisk the eggs, milk and seasonings together. Put a little butter in a nonstick frying pan and heat it on medium till it foams. Add the eggs and scramble them till they are starting to set but still loose. Stir in the cheese and then spoon the eggs into the ham cups.

Bake the ham cups in the oven for 5 minutes, till the eggs are completely set. Remove the cups from the muffin tin and serve in small bowls, or line them up on a platter to serve.

My husband would say to serve ketchup with these, but I turn up my nose at that!

CHEF STELLINO'S
SUGGESTED WINE PAIRING: *Bodega Septima* Chardonnay

Chocolate-Dipped Cake Lollipops

GALE GAND

Makes approximately 16 lollipops

2 cups cake crumbs (See recipe instructions.)
¼ cup frosting, in the flavor of your choice
16 8-inch lollipop sticks, available at craft stores
Assorted sprinkles, sanding sugar, chopped nuts
12 ounces semisweet chocolate
3 ounces white chocolate (optional, for drizzling on the lollipops)

Break up a cake to make crumbs. Add the frosting and mix until the crumbs hold together. Roll the crumbs in your hand to form a ball. Place the rolled balls onto a sheet pan and insert a lollipop stick into the center of each. Freeze these for 1 hour. (You can freeze the balls for up to 30 days.)

Arrange a few ramekins containing your sprinkles, sanding sugar or other decorations next to a large piece of Styrofoam, which you will use for drying the dipped lollipops. Place the semisweet chocolate and optional white chocolate into separate mixing bowls (making sure the bowls are dry), and melt over barely simmering water. Stir the chocolate to ensure even melting.

When the chocolate is melted, remove it from the water bath. Dip each lollipop into the semisweet chocolate just until the ball (but not the stick) is covered. Lift the lollipop out of the chocolate and slowly spin it for about 30 seconds. Lightly press the top of the pop into the selected topping(s) or drizzle with melted white chocolate.

Push the end of each lollipop stick into the Styrofoam and allow the pops to set for about 20 minutes. Then place in a container, with paper between the layers. Refrigerate for up to 7 days.

Banana Cream Pie Spoons

GALE GAND

Makes 50 servings

FOR THE PIE-DOUGH TRIANGLES:
3 ounces cold unsalted butter
3 ounces shortening, frozen
1 ice cube
½ cup water
1 teaspoon Pompeian® Red Wine Vinegar
2¼ cups all-purpose flour, plus extra for dusting the work surface
1 teaspoon kosher salt
1 teaspoon C&H® or Domino® Sugar, plus extra for brushing the dough
Cream, for brushing the dough

FOR THE CUSTARD:
2 cups milk (whole, 2% reduced-fat or 1% lowfat)
½ vanilla bean, split lengthwise
6 egg yolks
⅔ cup C&H® or Domino® Sugar
¼ cup cornstarch
1 tablespoon unsalted butter

FOR THE GARNISH:
2 cups heavy cream
2 teaspoons C&H® or Domino® Sugar
5 bananas, sliced

TO PREPARE THE PIE-DOUGH TRIANGLES:

Cut the chilled butter into small cubes and refrigerate while you prepare the shortening. Use a rubber spatula to spread the shortening about ¼ inch thick on a piece of foil (about a 6-inch square). Score the shortening with the edge of the rubber spatula to make a grid of ½-inch squares, and then freeze it. When this is chilled and hardened, you will have cubes of shortening.

Place an ice cube in a 1-cup measuring cup, add enough water to bring it up to ½ cup, then add the vinegar. Set aside to chill the water until ice cold, and to melt the ice.

In the bowl of a stand mixer fitted with a paddle attachment, place the flour, salt, sugar, chilled butter and frozen shortening (bend the foil back to release the shortening from the foil), and mix on low until the butter and shortening pieces are the size of large peas. Add the ice water-vinegar mixture. Turn the mixer to medium-low speed and count just to 25, to avoid overmixing the dough, then turn the mixer off. Form the dough into 2 disks and refrigerate for at least 2 hours, or overnight.

Working on a floured surface, use a rolling pin to roll out 1 disk of dough into a rectangle; the rolled-out dough should be ⅛ inch thick. Refrigerate that dough while you roll out the second disk of dough into another ⅛-inch-thick rectangle; place that dough in the refrigerator as well. The dough should be refrigerated just long enough to become firm again. Cut each sheet into strips about 1¼ inches wide, and then cut the strips into equilateral triangles that are about 1½ inches wide at the base. Keeping them close together, chill the triangles, then brush with cream and sugar.

Heat the oven to 400 degrees. Spread the triangles out on a sheet pan and bake till light golden brown. Let cool on the pan. Store in an airtight container.

TO PREPARE THE CUSTARD:

In a medium saucepan, heat the milk and vanilla bean to a boil over medium heat. Immediately turn off the heat and set aside to infuse for 10 to 15 minutes.

In a bowl (I usually do this in the bowl of a stand mixer with a whisk attachment), whisk the egg yolks and sugar until light and fluffy. Add the cornstarch and whisk vigorously until no lumps remain. Whisk in ¼ cup of the hot milk mixture until incorporated. Whisk in the remaining hot milk mixture, reserving the empty saucepan.

Pour the mixture through a strainer back into the saucepan. Cook over medium-high heat, whisking constantly, until thickened and slowly boiling. Remove from the heat and stir in the butter. Let cool slightly. Cover with plastic wrap, lightly pressing the plastic against the surface to prevent a skin from forming. Chill for at least 2 hours, or until ready to serve.

Make whipped cream for the garnish by whipping the cream with the sugar till stiff. Keep chilled.

TO SERVE:

Pipe the custard into spoons. Tuck 1 triangle of baked pie dough into the custard, place a banana slice on that, and pipe a small kiss of whipped cream on top of that.

CHEF STELLINO'S SUGGESTED WINE PAIRING: *Voga* Moscato

Tiramisù

NICK STELLINO

Serves 8 to 10

2½ cups strong coffee, cooled
½ cup coffee liqueur
2 packages ladyfingers cookies
9 eggs, yolks and whites separated
1¾ cups C&H® or Domino® Sugar, divided
1½ pounds mascarpone cheese
1½ teaspoons vanilla extract
1 cup semisweet chocolate, finely chopped
½ cup sweet cocoa powder

Mix the cold coffee and the liqueur in a large bowl. In batches, dip the ladyfingers in the coffee mixture. You want them to be moist on the outside but still crunchy on the inside.

Beat the egg yolks with half of the sugar until the mixture is thick enough to form a long ribbon when you lift the beater out. (If you are concerned about using raw eggs, once you have beaten the egg yolks, cook them in a double boiler, whisking constantly until they become as thick as a custard cream. Be careful not to overcook them, or they will become scrambled eggs. After cooking the yolks, proceed with the recipe.) Add the mascarpone and beat for 2 to 3 more minutes. Set aside.

Beat the egg whites, adding the remaining sugar a bit at a time, until they form stiff peaks and have a glossy sheen, about 4 minutes.

Gently fold the egg whites into the mascarpone mixture until the mixture is all the same color. Add the vanilla and chopped semisweet chocolate, and gently fold them into the mixture.

In a 9-by-17-inch glass baking dish, assemble the dessert. Layer the bottom of the dish with the soaked cookies. Top with a layer of the mascarpone-chocolate mixture. Repeat the procedure to make 1 more layer.

Using a flour sifter, cover the top of the tiramisù with a thin layer of sweet cocoa powder. Place the tiramisù in the refrigerator and let it rest for at least 5 hours; it's even better if refrigerated overnight. Serve it with pride! For an extra treat, top with Salsa di Fragole (Strawberry Sauce). See recipe on next page.

CHEF'S TIP: You may notice that there's enough of the mixture left over to make an additional, smaller tiramisù. This usually doesn't happen to me, because I keep tasting to make sure that there is enough sugar and chocolate. By the time I am done, there is enough for only one pan. Don't laugh—it might happen to you, too!

CHEF STELLINO'S SUGGESTED WINE PAIRING: *Artesa* Artisan Series Orange Muscat

Strawberry Sauce
Salsa di Fragole

NICK STELLINO

Yields 1 cup

1 10-ounce package whole frozen strawberries, partially thawed
2 tablespoons crème de cassis liqueur
¼ cup C&H® or Domino® Sugar

Place the frozen strawberries in a food processor. Add the cassis and sugar. Pulse until pureed. Taste.

If the texture of the strawberry seeds bothers you, strain through a fine-mesh strainer or cheesecloth-like strainer to remove the seeds; otherwise, it is ready to serve.

Chef Maria Hines
Tilth | Seattle

Yams with Meringue
Eggplant Ratatouille with Lemon-Marinated Chicken Breasts
Butternut Squash Risotto
Plums Two Ways with Pound Cake
Ozette Potato Salad

NS Pasta with Braised Sausages & Ricotta Parmigiana
Tomato Sauce

Yams with Meringue

MARIA HINES

Serves 4

FOR THE YAMS:
4 yams
Pompeian® Extra Virgin Olive Oil
Salt and pepper
2 sprigs fresh thyme, chopped
½ cup C&H® Golden Brown Sugar or Domino® Light Brown Sugar

FOR THE MERINGUE:
10 egg whites
1½ cups C&H® or Domino® Sugar
2 teaspoons vanilla extract
2 teaspoons cream of tartar

TO PREPARE THE YAMS:
Toss the yams with olive oil, salt and pepper. Roast the yams whole in the oven at 350 degrees until tender, 30 to 40 minutes.

Peel the skin off with a paring knife while the yams are warm. Slice the yams into thin coins. Toss them with salt, pepper, chopped fresh thyme and brown sugar.

Lay the yams in a square Pyrex® baking dish and, using a pastry bag, cover them with the meringue. Put them under the broiler just long enough to brown the top of the meringue.

TO PREPARE THE MERINGUE:
Combine the egg whites, sugar, vanilla and cream of tartar in a bain-marie. Whisk the mixture constantly to avoid cooking the eggs. Remove once the mixture is hot to the touch (5 to 7 minutes).

Transfer the bowl to a small mixer and, using the whisk attachment, mix on low speed, gradually increasing to high speed until stiff, glossy peaks form (about 10 minutes).

**CHEF STELLINO'S
SUGGESTED WINE PAIRING:** *Voga* Sparkling Pinot Grigio

Eggplant Ratatouille with Lemon-Marinated Chicken Breasts

MARIA HINES

Serves 4

Juice of ½ lemon
¼ cup Pompeian® Extra Virgin Olive Oil
Kosher salt and freshly ground black pepper to taste
1 clove garlic, minced
4 chicken breasts

FOR THE RATATOUILLE:
3 tablespoons Pompeian® Extra Virgin Olive Oil
2 cloves garlic, minced
1 medium yellow onion, cut into ¼-inch dice
1 large purple eggplant, peeled and cut into ¼-inch dice
2 small zucchini, cut into ¼-inch dice
1 medium to large green bell pepper, cut into ¼-inch dice
1 cup sundried tomatoes packed in olive oil (see Chef's Tips), cut into ¼-inch dice
Kosher salt and freshly ground black pepper to taste
½ cup Artesa Carneros Chardonnay
1 to 2 teaspoons white wine vinegar or Pompeian® Pomegranate Infused White Balsamic Vinegar
¼ cup chopped flat-leaf parsley

In a small bowl, whisk together the lemon juice, olive oil, salt and pepper, and garlic. Place the chicken breasts in a small baking dish or a large zipper bag. Add the lemon mixture and coat the chicken thoroughly. Set aside.

Preheat the grill for direct heat.

TO PREPARE THE RATATOUILLE:
In a large pan, heat 3 tablespoons olive oil over medium heat. Add the garlic and onion, and sauté until the onion starts to soften, about 1 to 2 minutes. Add the eggplant, zucchini, bell pepper and tomatoes. Stir to combine. Season with salt and black pepper. Cover the pan with a lid and let cook for about 20 minutes, stirring frequently.

Remove the chicken from the marinade; discard the marinade. Place the chicken on the grill and grill for about 3 to 5 minutes per side, or until done. Remove from the grill.

To finish the ratatouille, add the Chardonnay and stir to combine. Let the wine cook off, gently scraping the pan to deglaze it. Taste, and adjust the seasoning by adding salt and pepper to taste. Add 1 or 2 teaspoons vinegar. Add the parsley and give the ratatouille a final stir.

Spoon the ratatouille onto 4 plates. Add the chicken breasts and serve.

CHEF'S TIPS: If you can't find sundried tomatoes packed in olive oil, use 4 Roma tomatoes (or an equivalent amount of another variety), seeded and diced.

Ratatouille can be served cold and paired with cold meats—perfect for the day after if you don't feel like cooking.

It's hard for the body to digest the cellulose in raw onions, so it's always better to eat cooked onions.

**CHEF STELLINO'S
SUGGESTED WINE PAIRING:** *Artesa* Estate Reserve Pinot Noir

Butternut Squash Risotto

MARIA HINES

Serves 4

¼ cup unsalted butter, divided
½ yellow onion, minced to the same size as the rice
1 teaspoon minced garlic
¼ cup Artesa Carneros Chardonnay
2 cups Carnaroli rice
8 cups vegetable stock
⅛ cup finely grated Parmesan
2 tablespoons toasted pine nuts
1 cup butternut squash, cut into ¼-inch dice, then blanched for 30 seconds
½ teaspoon kosher salt
1 teaspoon pepper
¼ of a lemon
1 tablespoon parsley, chopped

Heat a shallow sauté pan on medium-high. Add half of the ¼ cup of unsalted butter to the pan with the yellow onion and garlic. Sweat the onion and garlic until they turn translucent, then add the Chardonnay. Add your rice and begin to toast it gently.

Meanwhile, place your vegetable stock in a saucepan over high heat. Start adding stock, 1 6-ounce ladleful at a time, to the risotto while stirring constantly. (By stirring, you're going to release the natural starches.) Reserve 1 ladleful of stock.

Keep tasting your risotto until it is at your desired texture. At this point, take the risotto off the heat and add the reserved ladleful of stock, stirring it in. Also add the rest of your butter and the Parmesan, pine nuts and butternut squash. Season with salt and pepper and a squeeze of a quarter of a lemon. Garnish with lots of chopped parsley. Serve quickly and enjoy!

CHEF STELLINO'S SUGGESTED WINE PAIRING: *Belmondo* Pinot Grigio

Chef Hines UNSCRIPTED

WHY DO YOU DO WHAT YOU DO?
 I love to cook!

WHAT IS YOUR FIRST FOOD MEMORY?
 Cleaning octopus with my mom when I was 5.

WHAT IS YOUR FAVORITE DISH TO EAT? TO PREPARE?
 I love duck confit!

IS THERE A FOOD YOU HATE/DON'T LIKE?
 I love everything.

IF YOU COULD HAVE ONLY ONE FOOD FOR THE REST OF YOUR LIFE, WHAT WOULD THAT FOOD BE?
 Chawan mush!

WHAT OR WHO INSPIRES YOU?
 Alice Waters.

Plums Two Ways with Pound Cake

MARIA HINES

Serves 4

1 loaf pound cake (store-bought is fine), **at room temperature**

FOR PLUM COMPOTE:
1 tablespoon butter
¼ teaspoon salt
8 plums, pitted and coarsely chopped
1 cup C&H® or Domino® Sugar, plus more as needed
1 tablespoon lemon juice

FOR PLUOT SALAD:
3 pluots, halved, pitted and sliced thinly
¼ cup mint leaves, cut chiffonade style (See Chef's Tips.)
Honey (preferably a light-flavored variety such as fireweed)

If it isn't already, let the pound cake come to room temperature.

TO PREPARE THE PLUM COMPOTE:
In a pot, melt the butter over medium-high heat. Add the salt and the chopped plums. Once the plums are warmed through, add the sugar and give it a stir to combine. Once the sugar has dissolved, add the lemon juice. Let simmer for about 2 minutes. Taste, and add a touch more sugar, if needed. You want to have a nice sweet-tart balance. Set aside.

TO PREPARE THE PLUOT SALAD:
Combine the sliced pluots and the mint. Toss to combine. Drizzle with honey (about 1 tablespoon), and toss gently to incorporate the honey.

TO SERVE:
Cut the pound cake into 1-inch-thick slices. Place on plates.

Spoon the compote on top of the cake. Spoon the pluot salad on the side.

CHEF'S TIPS: To cut the mint in chiffonade style, stack the mint leaves. Roll them into a cigar shape, starting at the tip and rolling toward the stem. Slice thinly.

There are many varieties of plums available at the farmers market, including Santa Rosa, Damson and Mirabelle. Taste before you buy. The tarter varieties will require a little more sugar during cooking. When buying plums, look for ones that are just right: not too soft and not too hard.

Ozette Potato Salad

MARIA HINES

Serves 4

2 pounds Ozette potatoes

1 tablespoon Dijon mustard
1 tablespoon whole-grain mustard
¼ cup apple cider vinegar or Pompeian® Pomegranate Infused White Balsamic Vinegar
½ cup mayonnaise
¼ cup finely chopped chives
¼ cup finely chopped parsley
Salt and pepper to taste
½ cup hazelnut oil, plus more as needed
1 clove shallot, minced
2 cloves garlic, minced

Put the potatoes in a large pot and add enough water to cover. Bring to a boil and let cook until they're tender enough that you can easily pierce the flesh, but don't overcook. Drain, and let cool for about 15 minutes.

In the meantime, create a seasoning mixture by combining the mustards, vinegar, mayonnaise, chives, parsley, salt and pepper to taste (you might need extra salt, because the potatoes will absorb it), and ½ cup hazelnut oil. Stir.

Slice the potatoes into coins about ¼ inch thick. Toss gently with the shallot, the garlic and the seasoning mixture. Taste, and adjust the seasoning as needed. Drizzle with additional hazelnut oil if the potatoes seem dry. Serve warm or at room temperature.

CHEF STELLINO'S SUGGESTED WINE PAIRING: *Legaris* Verdejo

Pound Cake (OPPOSITE PAGE)
Anna de Codorníu Brut Rosé

Pasta with Braised Sausages & Ricotta Parmigiana

NICK STELLINO

Serves 4

3 cups Tomato Sauce (See recipe on page 89.)
1 pound spicy Italian sausages, removed from the casing and cut into 1-inch pieces
4 tablespoons freshly chopped basil, divided
1 pound ricotta cheese
1 cup grated Parmesan cheese, divided
1 teaspoon black pepper
1 pound DaVinci® pasta—spaghetti or penne rigate

Bring 3 cups of tomato sauce to a simmer over medium heat and add the sausage and half of the chopped basil. Stir well and cook for 30 minutes.

While the sauce is cooking, pour the ricotta into a strainer over a stainless-steel bowl, and let it drain for 15 minutes.

Dispose of the liquid that has accumulated at the bottom of the bowl, and mix the ricotta cheese left in the strainer with ½ cup of the grated Parmesan and 1 teaspoon of black pepper. Set the ricotta-Parmesan mixture aside.

Cook the pasta in a pot of boiling water for 10 minutes. Drain it well, return it to the pot, and pour about 2 cups of the sauce-and-sausage mixture over it. Cook for 3 more minutes over medium-low heat, stirring well.

Serve the pasta in individual bowls, sprinkle with the remaining chopped basil, and top with a large dollop of the ricotta-Parmesan mixture. Bring to the table with the remaining sauce and the remaining grated Parmesan.

CHEF'S TIP: For a creamier look, pour half of the ricotta-Parmesan mixture over the cooked pasta and the sauce in the pot, then serve with just grated cheese and chopped basil on top of it.

CHEF STELLINO'S SUGGESTED WINE PAIRING: *Elements by Artesa* Cabernet Sauvignon

"All the best moments of my life include tomato sauce, in one form or another!"

Tomato Sauce
Sugo di Pomodoro

NICK STELLINO

Yields 7½ cups

8 tablespoons Pompeian® Extra Virgin Olive Oil
6 garlic cloves
2 cups onion, chopped
1½ teaspoons red pepper flakes
3 28-ounce cans Italian crushed tomatoes
½ teaspoon salt
½ teaspoon pepper
½ tablespoon C&H® or Domino® Sugar (optional)
8 tablespoons fresh basil, chopped, or 2½ teaspoons dried
½ teaspoon dried oregano

Pour the olive oil into a stockpot that holds at least 3 quarts. Add the garlic, onion and red pepper flakes, and cook over medium heat for 15 minutes, stirring often, until the onions start to brown.

Add the crushed tomatoes, salt, pepper, sugar (use sugar only if the tomatoes are tart), basil and oregano, and bring to a boil, then simmer for 35 to 40 minutes, stirring occasionally.

Use the sauce right away, store in the refrigerator for up to 3 days, or freeze for up to 1 month. Before you refrigerate or freeze it, let the sauce come to room temperature.

CHEF'S TIP: For a smoother, more elegant presentation, once the sauce is at room temperature, process it in batches in a food processor. The sauce will go through a slight change in color; the flavor, however, will not change.

Chef Andy Husbands
Tremont 647 & Sister Sorel | Boston

- The Ultimate Chocolate Chip Cookie
- Andy's First Place BBQ Glazed Pork Tenderloin with Bacon-Corn Relish & Cheddar Grits
- Lemon-Lime Bars
- Chicken Chicharrones with Fresh Oregano
- Limed Sour Cream
- Salsa 101

NS Arugula, Romaine & Radicchio Salad with Glazed Pine Nuts, Prosciutto Chips & Gorgonzola Dressing

The Ultimate Chocolate Chip Cookie

ANDY HUSBANDS

Makes 2 dozen large cookies

1¼ **cups all-purpose flour**
1 **cup quick-cooking oats, ground to powder in a food processor**
1 **(1.55-ounce) plain chocolate candy bar, chilled and ground to powder in a food processor**
1 **teaspoon baking soda**
1 **teaspoon kosher salt**
1 **cup** (2 sticks) **unsalted butter, softened**
½ **cup C&H® or Domino® Sugar**
½ **cup packed C&H® Golden Brown Sugar or Domino® Light Brown Sugar**
1 **large egg**
½ **teaspoon vanilla extract**
¾ **cup bittersweet or semisweet chocolate chips**
½ **cup toasted and chopped almonds or pecans**

Preheat the oven to 350 degrees.

In a large mixing bowl, stir together the flour, oat powder, ground candy bar, baking soda and salt.

In the large bowl of an electric mixer, cream together the butter, granulated sugar and brown sugar until well blended and fluffy. Add the egg and vanilla, and mix until combined. Add the flour mixture in 3 additions, mixing until incorporated and scraping down the sides of the bowl after each addition. Fold in the chocolate chips and nuts.

Use a large spoon to drop 2-inch mounds of dough about 3 inches apart on an ungreased baking sheet. Bake until the edges of the cookies are golden brown and the centers start to color, 10 to 12 minutes. Remove from the oven and let cool on the baking sheet for 2 minutes, then transfer to a cooling rack.

**CHEF STELLINO
SUGGESTS PAIRING WITH:** *Amarula* Cream Liqueur

Andy's First Place BBQ Glazed Pork Tenderloin
with Bacon-Corn Relish & Cheddar Grits

ANDY HUSBANDS

Serves 4 to 6 as an entrée

FOR ANDY'S FIRST PLACE BBQ GLAZE (YIELDS ABOUT 4 CUPS):

¾ cup C&H® Golden Brown Sugar or Domino® Light Brown Sugar
¼ cup cider vinegar or Pompeian® Pomegranate Infused White Balsamic Vinegar
3 tablespoons Worcestershire sauce
¼ cup Dijon mustard
1½ tablespoons Pompeian® Pomegranate Infused White Balsamic Vinegar
2 teaspoons mustard powder
1 teaspoon cumin seeds, toasted and coarsely ground
1 tablespoon curry powder
2 cups ketchup
1 teaspoon dried marjoram

FOR THE PORK TENDERLOIN:

1 cup, lightly packed, fresh basil leaves
2 cloves garlic, peeled
2 tablespoons cider vinegar or Pompeian® Pomegranate Infused White Balsamic Vinegar
2 tablespoons Pompeian® Extra Virgin Olive Oil
Salt and freshly ground black pepper to taste
2 (1- to 1½-pound) **pork tenderloins**
1 recipe Andy's First Place BBQ Glaze

FOR THE BACON-CORN RELISH:

1 cup fresh corn kernels (about 2 large ears)
2 tablespoons fresh-squeezed lemon juice (about ½ lemon)
½ small red onion, peeled and cut into ¼-inch dice
1 tablespoon Pompeian® Extra Virgin Olive Oil
¼ cup green olives, pitted and chopped
¼ cup flat-leaf Italian parsley, chopped
½ cup bacon bits
2 tablespoons chives, minced
Salt and freshly ground black pepper to taste

FOR THE CHEDDAR GRITS:
1 tablespoon butter
2 cloves garlic, peeled and minced
¾ cup water
¾ cup whole milk
¾ cup instant grits
¼ cup sharp Vermont Cheddar, shredded
3 tablespoons mascarpone cheese
Salt and freshly ground black pepper to taste

TO PREPARE ANDY'S FIRST PLACE BBQ GLAZE:
Combine all of the ingredients in a small, heavy-bottomed 2-quart saucepan over low heat. Whisk until entirely incorporated and simmer for 30 minutes, stirring occasionally. Use hot or cold.

TO PREPARE THE PORK TENDERLOIN:
Preheat the oven to 425 degrees.

In a food processor or blender, combine the basil, garlic, cider vinegar or pomegranate infused white balsamic, and extra virgin olive oil; puree, and season with salt and pepper. Rub the mixture into the pork tenderloins, coating them completely.

Heat a large, heavy-bottomed ovenproof sauté pan over high heat. Sear the pork until browned on all sides, 2 to 4 minutes. Transfer the pan to the oven and roast the tenderloins to an internal temperature of 135 degrees, 10 to 15 minutes. While the pork is roasting, make the bacon-corn relish and Cheddar grits.

TO PREPARE THE BACON-CORN RELISH:
Combine the corn, lemon juice, onion, extra virgin olive oil, olives, parsley, bacon bits and chives, and season generously with salt and pepper.

TO PREPARE THE CHEDDAR GRITS:
Place the butter and garlic in a heavy-bottomed 1-quart saucepan over medium heat and cook, stirring frequently, until the garlic is fragrant, approximately ½ minute. Add the water and milk, increase the heat to medium-high, and continue cooking until the liquid starts to simmer, approximately ½ minute. Slowly whisk in the grits, and simmer, stirring occasionally, for 3 to 4 minutes. Stir in the Cheddar and mascarpone, and season with salt and freshly ground black pepper to taste. Serve immediately.

TO SERVE:
When the pork is done, remove from the oven and brush with the BBQ glaze. Transfer to a cutting board and allow to rest for 5 minutes. Slice crosswise into ¼-inch-thick pieces, and arrange overlapping slices on a platter. Spoon some of the bacon-corn relish over the pork, and pass the remaining relish on the side. Serve the Cheddar grits with the pork.

CHEF STELLINO'S SUGGESTED WINE PAIRING: *Elements by Artesa* Red Wine

Lemon-Lime Bars

ANDY HUSBANDS

Makes 24 bars

2¼ cups all-purpose flour, divided
½ cup C&H® Powdered Sugar or Domino® Confectioners Sugar, plus extra for dusting
¼ teaspoon kosher salt
1 cup (2 sticks) unsalted butter, softened
4 large eggs
2 cups C&H® or Domino® Sugar
2 teaspoons finely grated lemon zest
2 teaspoons finely grated lime zest
2 tablespoons fresh lemon juice (about ½ large lemon)
2 tablespoons fresh lime juice (about 1 large lime)
2 teaspoons ground ginger

Preheat the oven to 350 degrees.

In the large bowl of an electric mixer, sift together 2 cups of the flour, the powdered/confectioners sugar and the salt. Add the butter, and mix on low speed until thoroughly combined but not creamy. Press evenly into the bottom of an ungreased 9-by-13-inch baking pan. Bake until pale golden, about 25 minutes. Let cool to room temperature.

While the crust is cooling, beat the eggs in another large mixing bowl. Add the granulated sugar, lemon and lime zest, lemon and lime juice and ground ginger, and the remaining ¼ cup flour; whisk until thoroughly combined. Pour over the cooled crust.

Reduce the oven temperature to 325 degrees and bake until firm, 35 to 40 minutes. Remove from the oven and run a knife around the edge of the pan to loosen. Allow to cool completely, and dust with powdered/confectioners sugar. Cut into bars, and serve.

CHEF STELLINO SUGGESTS PAIRING WITH: *Amarula* Cream Liqueur

Chef Husbands UNSCRIPTED

WHY DO YOU DO WHAT YOU DO?

I've always had a passion for cooking. In fourth grade, I did a demo of how to make donuts. Ironically, donuts are a mainstay of my menu so many years later. Multitasking and creativity at the same time is a rush that feeds my desire to do more.

WHAT IS YOUR FIRST FOOD MEMORY?

When I was in first grade, I remember my mom used to make popovers with tuna fish salad on the side. I loved how gooey yet crunchy they were, and so warm... To this day, eating popovers still reminds me of being a kid.

WHAT IS YOUR FAVORITE DISH TO EAT? TO PREPARE?

I like to cook with the seasons, so instead of a favorite dish, I simply prefer to go to the markets and buy what's fresh and local, and cook from there. My style is always big and complex flavors, so I inject this into what I find at the market.

IS THERE A FOOD YOU HATE/DON'T LIKE?

I've traveled all over the world and will try anything once. In Mexico, I wasn't fond of the intestines in chile sauce. (The sauce was amazing, but the intestines were a little rubbery and not yummy.) I try not to hate on food and give everything a chance.

IF YOU COULD HAVE ONLY ONE FOOD FOR THE REST OF YOUR LIFE, WHAT WOULD THAT FOOD BE?

Pork—so versatile and delicious...from bacon to the tail...I'd live a happy life.

WHAT OR WHO INSPIRES YOU?

The seasons are my main inspiration. I'm a student of food history, and I love reading old cookbooks. By looking backwards, you can see the future and what's to come.

Chicken Chicharrones with Fresh Oregano

ANDY HUSBANDS

Serves 4 as an appetizer or 2 as an entrée

These little nuggets of crispy, moist chicken are best eaten scooped up in a warm tortilla and drizzled with Limed Sour Cream. (See recipe on page 99.) The secret to the texture lies in the high heat; the meat comes awfully close to burning, so be prepared to act quickly.

¼ cup Pompeian® Extra Light Tasting Olive Oil
1½ pounds skinless, boneless chicken thighs, cut into 3-inch squares
Kosher salt and freshly cracked black pepper to taste
¼ cup peeled and minced garlic
1 tablespoon chili powder
1 tablespoon cumin seeds, toasted and ground
1 tablespoon coriander seeds, toasted and ground
1 tablespoon fresh oregano, roughly chopped
⅓ cup Pompeian® Pomegranate Infused White Balsamic Vinegar
½ lime, cut into wedges

In a heavy-bottomed skillet over medium-high heat, heat the olive oil until it is hot but not smoking.

Season the chicken with salt and pepper, and add it to the skillet. Cook until it turns golden brown and starts to fall apart, 7 to 10 minutes, stirring occasionally and scraping as it sticks to the bottom of the pan.

Add the garlic and cook 2 more minutes, stirring constantly so the garlic doesn't burn. Add the chili powder, cumin, coriander and oregano; cook for 1 minute. Stir in the vinegar and cook until the chicken is glazed, about 1 minute more. Remove from the heat. Season with salt and pepper.

Squeeze the fresh lime over the chicken and serve hot with warm tortillas, Salsa 101 and Limed Sour Cream. (See recipes on page 99.)

**CHEF STELLINO'S
SUGGESTED WINE PAIRING:** *Two Oceans* Sauvignon Blanc

Limed Sour Cream

ANDY HUSBANDS

Makes about ½ cup

A classic condiment made muy picante (that's "very spicy," for the English-only crowd) by the addition of cumin, chipotle and, of course, lime. Serve straight up with chips and salsa, or with grilled or roasted chicken, grilled shrimp, or any Latin-style dish, such as Chicken Chicharrones with Fresh Oregano. (See recipe on page 98.)

½ cup sour cream
Juice of 1 lime (about 2 tablespoons)
½ teaspoon cumin seeds, toasted and ground
1 dried chipotle pepper, rehydrated and minced (squeezed of extra liquid if canned)
Salt and freshly cracked black pepper to taste

Combine all the ingredients in a small mixing bowl and stir thoroughly.

This condiment will keep for about 1 week refrigerated in an airtight container.

Salsa 101

ANDY HUSBANDS

Makes about 2 cups

Salsa hasn't been exotic in years; it's more popular than ketchup. Too many people, though, eat it out of a jar, not realizing that nothing compares to a fresh salsa. What's the upside to that? Even though it's simple to make, your guests will be instantly impressed.

1 large, ripe tomato, cut into ¼-inch dice
½ cup red onion, minced
½ cup cilantro, chopped
1 jalapeño, seeded and minced
2 tablespoons freshly squeezed lime juice (about 1 lime)
1 tablespoon Pompeian® Extra Virgin Olive Oil
Salt and freshly ground black pepper to taste

In a medium-sized mixing bowl, combine all the ingredients.

The salsa will keep for up to 1 week refrigerated.

Arugula, Romaine & Radicchio Salad
with Glazed Pine Nuts, Prosciutto Chips & Gorgonzola Dressing

NICK STELLINO

Serves 4

4 ounces baby arugula salad
4 ounces heart of romaine, cut into ½-inch pieces
4 ounces radicchio, cut into ½-inch pieces
Gorgonzola dressing (See accompanying recipe.)
Prosciutto chips (See accompanying recipe.)
4 ounces crumbled Gorgonzola cheese
Parmesan-glazed pine nuts (See accompanying recipe.)

FOR THE GORGONZOLA DRESSING:
3 ounces Gorgonzola cheese
2 tablespoons Pompeian® Pomegranate Infused White Balsamic Vinegar
6 tablespoons Pompeian® Extra Virgin Olive Oil
½ teaspoon salt
½ teaspoon C&H® or Domino® Sugar
½ teaspoon ground pepper

FOR THE PROSCIUTTO CHIPS:
½ teaspoon Pompeian® Extra Virgin Olive Oil
3 ounces prosciutto, thinly sliced

FOR THE PARMESAN-GLAZED PINE NUTS:
½ teaspoon Pompeian® Extra Virgin Olive Oil
½ cup pine nuts
2 tablespoons grated Parmesan cheese

TO PREPARE THE GORGONZOLA DRESSING:
Place all the ingredients into a food processor and process for about a minute until the dressing reaches a smooth, cream-like consistency.

TO PREPARE THE PROSCIUTTO CHIPS:
Add the olive oil to a large nonstick sauté pan and cook over medium-high heat. As the oil starts to sizzle, reduce the heat to medium and add the slices of prosciutto to the pan. Reduce the heat to medium-low and cook the prosciutto slices for a total of 4 minutes, about 2 minutes per side.

Place the prosciutto slices on a plate lined with absorbent paper and let them come to room temperature. When they're cool enough to handle, break them into small pieces about ¼ inch in size; they will look like little chips.

TO PREPARE THE PARMESAN-GLAZED PINE NUTS:
Preheat the oil over high heat until sizzling.

Turn off the heat and add the pine nuts, stirring well until they start to brown, about 1 to 2 minutes.

Place the toasted pine nuts in a bowl and add the Parmesan, stirring well until it is all melted. Let the pine nuts cool to room temperature.

TO ASSEMBLE THE SALAD:
Combine the baby arugula, romaine and radicchio, and dress with half of the Gorgonzola dressing.

Place the salad in serving dishes and top with the prosciutto chips, crumbled Gorgonzola and glazed pine nuts, then drizzle with the remaining dressing and serve.

CHEF STELLINO'S SUGGESTED WINE PAIRING: *Artesa* Carneros Pinot Noir

"I love everything about radicchio—the color, the taste, the way it elevates any salad mix.

I love saying the word *radicchio*; it always makes me smile!"

Chef Rick Moonen
rm seafood | Las Vegas

Chilled English Pea Soup with Jumbo Lump Crab
Asparagus & Black Trumpet Mushroom Risotto with Truffle Foam
Rick's New England Clam Chowder
Almond Pound Cake with Strawberries & Mascarpone Cream
Fluke with Potato Gnocchi, Fava Beans & Mustard Sauce
Poached Calamari Ceviche

NS Andrew's Mac & Cheese
Nick's Chili-Spiced Burgers

Chilled English Pea Soup with Jumbo Lump Crab

RICK MOONEN

Makes 4 appetizer portions

FOR THE PEA SOUP:
2 cups freshly shucked English peas
1 quart ice water
Salt and pepper to taste

FOR THE CRABMEAT GARNISH:
4 ounces jumbo lump crabmeat, cleaned
1 tablespoon fresh mint, chiffonade
1 tablespoon fresh-squeezed lime juice
2 tablespoons Pompeian® Extra Virgin Olive Oil
Salt and pepper to taste
½ cup pea shoots, cleaned

TO PREPARE THE PEA SOUP:
In a large stainless-steel pot, bring 1 gallon of salted water to a rapid boil. Blanch the peas until they are just tender (approximately 1 minute). Transfer the peas to salted ice water immediately to stop the cooking and lock in the color.

Puree the peas in a blender on low speed. Add enough cold water to achieve a smooth consistency. Adjust the seasoning with salt and pepper, and strain through a china cap. Keep cold.

TO PREPARE THE CRABMEAT GARNISH:
Carefully check the crabmeat for tiny shells. Try not to break up the large pieces. In a small bowl, gently toss the crabmeat, mint, lime juice and olive oil. Taste, and season with salt and pepper.

Distribute the soup among 4 chilled bowls. Garnish each with a large tablespoon of the crab mixture. Garnish with the pea shoots.

CHEF STELLINO'S SUGGESTED WINE PAIRING: *Terras Gauda* O Rosal

Asparagus & Black Trumpet Mushroom Risotto with Truffle Foam

RICK MOONEN

Makes 6 appetizer portions

FOR THE RISOTTO:
3 tablespoons butter
2 tablespoons Pompeian® Extra Virgin Olive Oil
1 large onion, finely diced
4 cloves garlic
1 pound Arborio rice
2 cups Artesa Carneros Chardonnay
Salt and pepper to taste
6 cups vegetable stock, simmering

FOR THE ASPARAGUS GARNISH:
9 spears asparagus, blanched and shocked in salted water
1 pint black trumpet mushrooms, thoroughly cleaned and rinsed
1 tablespoon Pompeian® Extra Virgin Olive Oil
Salt and pepper to taste

FOR THE TRUFFLE FOAM:
1 cup concentrated mushroom stock
2 large shallots, finely diced
2 tablespoons truffle butter
½ cup heavy cream
Salt and pepper to taste

1 tablespoon truffle oil
3 tablespoons chives, chopped

TO PREPARE THE RISOTTO:
In a medium-sized stainless-steel pot, melt the butter with 2 tablespoons olive oil over medium heat. Add the onions and garlic, and cook until translucent. Add the rice and stir for 2 minutes to allow the rice to toast in the oil and butter. Add the Chardonnay and continue stirring until the liquid is absorbed. Season with salt and pepper.

Add the vegetable stock, 1 cup at a time, allowing the rice to absorb the liquid each time before adding the next cup. Continue adding the stock until the risotto mixture is creamy and the rice still has a slight bite.

TO PREPARE THE ASPARAGUS GARNISH:

Slice the blanched asparagus on the bias into 1-inch pieces. Sauté the trumpet mushrooms in 1 tablespoon olive oil over high heat in a sauté pan for 1 minute. Season with salt and pepper. Toss in the asparagus to warm it through.

TO PREPARE THE TRUFFLE FOAM:

In a small stainless-steel sauce pot, bring the mushroom stock to a simmer with the shallots. Transfer this mixture to a blender. With the motor running, add the truffle butter, cream, salt and pepper. Put this mixture back into the sauce pot.

TO FINISH:

Fold the hot garnish into the risotto and divide among 6 hot bowls. With an immersion blender, aerate the mushroom stock mixture until it foams. Spoon the foam over the risotto and drizzle with truffle oil. Sprinkle chopped chives over the top and serve.

CHEF STELLINO'S SUGGESTED WINE PAIRING: *Piccini* Sasso al Poggio

"This slightly smoky version is based on the traditional, but would make a New England purist very upset."

Rick's New England Clam Chowder

RICK MOONEN

Serves 6

18 top neck clams
1 pint clam juice
2 tablespoons butter
6 strips bacon, cut into small pieces
1 medium onion, cut into medium dice
2 stalks celery, cut into medium dice
1 medium carrot, cut into medium dice
1 sachet (2 cloves garlic, a handful of parsley stems, 1 bay leaf, and a pinch each of salt and white pepper)
1 large leek, cut into medium dice
Salt and pepper to taste
½ cup flour
1 cup Artesa Carneros Chardonnay
3 medium red russet potatoes, cut into medium dice
1½ cups heavy cream
½ cup chives, dill and parsley, mixed
Juice of ½ lemon

Scrub the clams thoroughly under cold running water and place in a large pot with 1 cup of boiling water. Cover the pot and steam the clams for about 5 minutes, or just until they begin to open. Strain the liquid into a separate bowl and reserve. Remove the cooked meat from the clams and cut into medium chunks. Cover the cut clams with the pint of clam juice, and refrigerate.

Using the same pot that was used for the clams, over medium heat add the butter and bacon. Cook for 1 minute to melt the bacon fat. Add the onions, celery, carrots and sachet. Cover the pot and sweat the vegetables for 2 to 3 minutes. Add the leeks and sweat for 1 more minute. Season with salt and pepper.

Stir in the flour to coat the vegetables. Continue stirring for 2 minutes to cook the flour. DO NOT BROWN. Add the wine and simmer for 2 minutes. Carefully add the reserved clam liquid, making sure not to pour in any sand that may have settled on the bottom of the bowl. Add the potatoes, and let the chowder simmer for 10 minutes. Remove the pot from the heat and let the soup rest for half an hour. This allows the flavors to develop.

After the soup has rested, remove the sachet. When you are ready to serve the soup, return the pot to medium heat, add the cream, and bring to a simmer. Fold in the cut clams and mixed herbs. Season with a few squirts of lemon juice, and salt and pepper. Enjoy!

CHEF STELLINO'S SUGGESTED WINE PAIRING: *Artesa* Estate Reserve Chardonnay

Almond Pound Cake
with Strawberries & Mascarpone Cream

RICK MOONEN

Serves 6 to 8

FOR THE CAKE:
6 eggs
2 cups C&H® or Domino® Sugar
1 tablespoon orange zest
4 tablespoons orange juice
¾ cup crème fraîche
1¾ cups almond flour
1 cup all-purpose flour
¾ teaspoon baking powder
Pinch of salt
1 stick butter, melted and cooled

FOR THE MACERATED STRAWBERRIES:
2 pints strawberries
⅓ cup C&H® or Domino® Sugar

FOR THE MASCARPONE CREAM:
½ vanilla bean
1 cup mascarpone
1 cup heavy cream
¼ cup C&H® or Domino® Sugar

Pompeian® Balsamic Vinegar (optional)

TO PREPARE THE CAKE:
Preheat the oven to 350 degrees.

Butter 1 loaf pan. In a large bowl, whip the eggs with the sugar until thickened, about 2 minutes. Combine the orange zest, juice and crème fraîche. Sift together the almond flour, all-purpose flour, baking powder and salt.

Quickly add the juice mixture to the egg mixture and whisk for a few seconds, until just combined. With a rubber spatula, fold the dry ingredients into the liquids. Lastly, carefully fold in the butter.

Pour the batter into a loaf pan until it's about three-quarters full, and bake until a toothpick inserted into the cake comes out clean, about 45 minutes to 1 hour. Do not disturb the cake by opening the oven door for the first 40 minutes of baking, to ensure it won't deflate. Let cool in the baking pan, then invert.

TO PREPARE THE MACERATED STRAWBERRIES:
Quarter the strawberries and toss with the sugar. Let rest, covered and refrigerated, at least 2 hours or overnight.

TO PREPARE THE MASCARPONE CREAM:
Scrape the seeds from the vanilla bean into a bowl. Add the rest of the ingredients and whip until the mixture forms stiff peaks.

TO ASSEMBLE:
Slice the pound cake, top with the strawberries, and finish with a dollop of the mascarpone cream. For a luxurious addition, drizzle with the balsamic vinegar.

CHEF STELLINO'S SUGGESTED WINE PAIRING: *Anna de Codorníu* Brut

Chef Moonen UNSCRIPTED

WHY DO YOU DO WHAT YOU DO?
I love the connection I have with the world and people...the privilege of working with great products, understanding where they come from and how they are produced, and finally turning them into a great dining experience. I preach to maintain a responsibility that comes along with this privilege. It does not get any more personal than that.

WHAT IS YOUR FIRST FOOD MEMORY?
As a young boy, I would vacation on Long Island with my family. I recall tasting my first raw clam that I dug up myself on the beach in Sag Harbor. It changed my world, as I could taste the smell and flavor of the salty ocean in my mouth.

WHAT IS YOUR FAVORITE DISH TO EAT? TO PREPARE?
I love to make soups at home...it is so grounding. I usually prepare much more than I can consume myself, so I also enjoy sharing it with my friends. Most of the enjoyment of cooking comes from turning other people on to what you discover and create.

IS THERE A FOOD YOU HATE/DON'T LIKE?
Raw lobster and shrimp have a slimy texture that makes me gag. I can't wrap my mind around sea cucumbers for the same reason.

IF YOU COULD HAVE ONLY ONE FOOD FOR THE REST OF YOUR LIFE, WHAT WOULD THAT FOOD BE?
Pork...bacon...ham...get the picture here? I also love a free-range chicken...

WHAT OR WHO INSPIRES YOU?
Eating in ethnic sections of Las Vegas refreshes my interest in eating. I enjoy Chinatown especially... always something new for me to try. It pushes the boundaries of my creative mind.

"This recipe has a few micro recipes attached, but the end result is well worth the effort. It works terrifically well with any white flatfish, so feel free to substitute your local fresh selection. Fluke, flounder, Petrale sole, any Pacific sole, halibut, farmed turbot… The possibilities are endless, and the final dish will make you look like a kitchen genius. Give it a try!"

Fluke with Potato Gnocchi, Fava Beans & Mustard Sauce

RICK MOONEN

Serves 4

4 ounces beurre monté (See accompanying recipe.)
Salt and white pepper to taste
2 cups potato gnocchi (See accompanying recipe.)
1½ cups fava beans, shucked and peeled
4 tablespoons braised leeks (See accompanying recipe.)
1½ cups mustard sauce (See accompanying recipe.)
4 teaspoons lemon juice

Pinch of micro mustard greens (available from specialty farmers)
½ teaspoon mustard oil, divided

FOR THE MUSTARD CAVIAR BASE:
½ cup mustard seeds
3 ounces champagne vinegar or Pompeian® Pomegranate Infused White Balsamic Vinegar
3 ounces C&H® or Domino® Sugar
1 cup Dijon mustard
1 cup whole-grain mustard

FOR THE BEURRE MONTÉ (YIELDS 6 OUNCES):
½ cup water, plus more as needed
6 shallots, peeled and sliced thin
1 pound unsalted butter, cut into ½-inch cubes

FOR THE MUSTARD SAUCE:
1 tablespoon mustard caviar base (See accompanying recipe.)
2 ounces beurre monté (See accompanying recipe.)
1 teaspoon lemon juice
Salt and pepper to taste

FOR THE GNOCCHI:
Sea salt
4 russet potatoes
1 to 2 eggs, whipped
1 tablespoon salt
All-purpose flour
¼ cup blending flour, such as Wondra®
Pompeian® Extra Virgin Olive Oil

FOR THE BRAISED LEEKS:
12 leeks (white and light green parts only), **cut into medium dice**
3 tablespoons water
¾ pound unsalted butter
Salt and pepper to taste

FOR THE FLUKE:
4 6-ounce portions fluke, fillets cut in half
Salt and white pepper to taste
¼ cup all-purpose flour
3 tablespoons Pompeian® Extra Light Tasting Olive Oil

TO PREPARE THE MUSTARD CAVIAR BASE:
Combine the mustard seeds, vinegar and sugar in a pot, bringing to a gentle simmer and cooking until the mustard seeds are tender, about 2 hours. Let cool, then add the Dijon and whole-grain mustards.

TO PREPARE THE BEURRE MONTÉ:
Boil the shallots in ½ cup water until totally cooked, about 30 minutes, adding water as necessary to keep the shallots submerged. Add the mixture to a blender and slowly add butter, 1 cube at a time, until totally incorporated.

TO PREPARE THE MUSTARD SAUCE:
Whisk together 1 tablespoon of mustard caviar base and 2 ounces of beurre monté. Season with lemon juice, salt and pepper.

TO PREPARE THE GNOCCHI:
Preheat the oven to 350 degrees.

Cover a sheet tray with sea salt and place the potatoes on top. Place in the oven and roast until tender, approximately 60 minutes. Remove from the oven. While the potatoes are still warm, peel (you may need to wear two layers of disposable gloves). Pass the potatoes through a ricer, then let them cool.

Weigh the potatoes. (One-fifth of this weight will be how much flour you will add.) Mix enough egg into the potatoes to bind—approximately 1 egg will bind 2 medium potatoes. Season with the tablespoon of salt.

Weigh out the all-purpose flour. Place in a bowl and make a well in the center. Add the potato mixture and incorporate. Don't overwork the dough!

Divide the dough into 8 small batches. Roll out each batch of dough, using the Wondra® to prevent it from sticking, into ½-inch-diameter cylinders. Cut into ½-inch pieces.

Boil the gnocchi in salted water until floating. Remove to a pan containing olive oil, and toss the gnocchi to coat.

TO PREPARE THE BRAISED LEEKS:
Combine all of the ingredients in a pot and cover. Slowly heat the mixture and braise until the leeks are tender, while maintaining their original color, approximately 30 minutes. (Do not boil!)

TO PREPARE THE FLUKE:
Season both sides of the fluke portions with salt and white pepper, and dredge in the flour. Shake off any excess flour. Add the oil to a sauté pan and bring to medium heat. Add the fish to the pan and sauté over medium heat until golden and crisp, about 2 to 3 minutes. Turn the fish over and cook an additional 10 to 15 seconds. Remove from the pan and lay out on a towel.

TO FINISH:
Place 4 ounces beurre monté in a small pot over medium heat. Season with salt and white pepper, and add the gnocchi, the uncooked fava beans and the braised leeks.

In a separate pot, warm the mustard sauce and finish to taste with a squeeze of lemon juice, and salt and white pepper.

TO SERVE:
Place the gnocchi in the center of a warm bowl. Make a circle around the gnocchi with the warm mustard sauce, and lay the fish over the top, stacking 1 piece on top of another.

Dress the mustard greens with ¼ teaspoon mustard oil, and salt and pepper, and place on top of the fish. Garnish the plate with the remaining mustard oil.

CHEF STELLINO'S SUGGESTED WINE PAIRING: *Ca'Montini* Pinot Grigio

Poached Calamari Ceviche

RICK MOONEN

Serves 4

1 quart court bouillon (see accompanying recipe), **for the poaching of the calamari**
1 pound fresh baby squid, cleaned and cut into thin rounds
1 large bowl of ice water, for shocking the calamari
3 ounces fresh lime juice
4 tablespoons Pompeian® Extra Virgin Olive Oil
1 hothouse cucumber, peeled, seeded and made into small balls with a small melon baller
1 red bell pepper, roasted, peeled, seeded and cut into small dice
1 yellow bell pepper, roasted, peeled, seeded and cut into small dice
1 tablespoon mint, chiffonade
1 tablespoon cilantro, chiffonade
Salt and pepper to taste

6 ounces ripe red seedless watermelon, cut into rounds or disks with a ring mold cutter
1 teaspoon chili oil
1 teaspoon mint oil
2 or 3 sprigs fresh cilantro (or micro cilantro), **for garnish**

FOR THE COURT BOUILLON:
1 gallon water
2 large onions, cut into medium dice
1 large carrot, cut into medium dice
2 stalks celery, sliced
2 whole lemons, cut in half
1 whole bay leaf
10 black peppercorns
Salt to taste

TO PREPARE THE COURT BOUILLON:
In a large pot, bring all of the court bouillon ingredients to a boil. Season well with salt and simmer for 20 minutes.

TO PREPARE THE CALAMARI CEVICHE:
Bring the court bouillon back to a boil and turn off the flame so the boiling liquid stops rolling. Gently poach the squid in the still-hot bouillon for 45 seconds, then quickly drain the squid, and shock it in the ice water.

Once the squid is cool, remove it from the ice water and drain it on a paper towel.

In a mixing bowl, whisk the lime juice and olive oil together in the same fashion that you would mix a vinaigrette, then add the cucumber balls, diced red and yellow peppers, and chopped mint and cilantro. Season with salt and pepper to taste and then toss the poached squid in the vinaigrette.

TO SERVE:
Place the watermelon disks in the center of your plate, and arrange the dressed squid on the disks. Spoon the cucumber-pepper vinaigrette around and over the squid and watermelon. Garnish with drops of chili and mint oil, then top with fresh cilantro sprigs.

CHEF STELLINO'S SUGGESTED WINE PAIRING: *The Spanish Quarter* Chardonnay-Albariño

"Somebody yelled, 'That's enough cheese!'

'No,' I said. 'Not for my Andrew's Mac & Cheese!'"

Andrew's Mac & Cheese

NICK STELLINO

Serves 4

1 pound DaVinci® pasta—elbow or penne rigate
2 tablespoons Pompeian® Extra Virgin Olive Oil

4 cups whole milk
¼ teaspoon freshly ground black pepper, plus additional to taste
1 bay leaf
1 white onion, chopped
Salt to taste
¼ teaspoon grated nutmeg
4 tablespoons butter
4 tablespoons all-purpose flour

CHEESE MIX:
5 ounces sharp provolone, grated
4 ounces Asiago, grated
4 ounces Gruyère (sharp Swiss cheese), grated
4 ounces mozzarella, shredded
4 ounces Parmesan, grated

2 teaspoons truffle oil
½ cup bread crumbs

Preheat the oven to 400 degrees.

Cook the pasta al dente, drain well, set aside, and mix with 2 tablespoons of extra virgin olive oil so that it does not stick.

TO PREPARE THE CHEESE-AND-BESCIAMELLA SAUCE (YIELDS ABOUT 2 CUPS):
In a medium saucepan, heat the milk, pepper, bay leaf, onions, salt and nutmeg until the milk is steaming. Remove the bay leaf.

In a medium saucepan, melt the butter. Sprinkle in the flour, and stir with a wooden spoon until well blended. Cook, stirring, for 2 to 3 minutes until golden brown. This thin paste is called a roux. Slowly pour the steaming milk into the roux, whisking constantly to prevent lumps. Continue stirring over medium heat for 3 to 6 minutes. When the mixture thickens, take it off the heat. Add the cheeses and truffle oil to the sauce. Mix well until the cheeses are melted into the sauce.

TO FINISH:
Mix the pasta with three-quarters of the cheese-and-besciamella sauce. Pour the pasta into a greased baking dish in 2 layers, topping each layer with a portion of the remaining sauce. Sprinkle the top with bread crumbs and cook in the oven for about 15 minutes.

Nick's Chili-Spiced Burgers

NICK STELLINO

Serves 4

FOR THE CHILI SPICE MIXTURE:
1½ teaspoons paprika
1½ teaspoons dried oregano
1½ teaspoons onion powder
1½ teaspoons chili powder
½ teaspoon cumin
½ teaspoon garlic powder
½ teaspoon cayenne
½ teaspoon red pepper flakes
½ teaspoon salt
½ teaspoon ground pepper

FOR THE HAMBURGER PATTIES:
2½ pounds ground beef with at least 15% fat content
1 recipe chili spice mixture
1 teaspoon Worcestershire sauce
2 LARGE shallots, finely chopped (about 8 tablespoons)

ACCOMPANIMENTS:
8 slices Cheddar cheese
8 slices cooked bacon
4 hamburger buns
4 pieces lettuce
4 ¼-inch-thick slices of tomatoes
4 tablespoons shallots, chopped

TO PREPARE THE CHILI SPICE MIXTURE:
Mix all the ingredients well and set aside in a bowl.

TO PREPARE THE HAMBURGER PATTIES:
Add the spice mixture and the Worcestershire sauce and shallots to the ground meat and shape it into 4 patties.

Cook on a preheated barbecue over medium heat—about 5 minutes for medium-rare, 6 minutes for medium and 8 minutes for well done.

TO FINISH:

In the last minute of cooking, place 2 slices of cheese and 2 slices of cooked bacon on top of each patty, and cook until the cheese starts to melt.

Place the cooked patties on buns. Assemble the hamburgers with the remaining accompaniments, and serve.

CHEF STELLINO'S SUGGESTED WINE PAIRING: *Elements by Artesa* Cabernet Sauvignon

Andrew's Mac & Cheese (PREVIOUS SPREAD)
Elements by Artesa Cabernet Sauvignon

Chef Brian Poor
Portland City Grill | Portland, Oregon

Champagne Oyster Stew
Garlic-Roasted Whole Dungeness Crab & Arugula-Fennel Salad
Brown Sugar-Brined, Stove Top-Smoked Wild Salmon
Red & Gold Beet Salad
Basil-Garlic Braised Manila Clams

NS Veal Milanese with Tomato Pesto, Salad & Shaved Parmesan

Champagne Oyster Stew

BRIAN POOR

Serves 3 to 4

2 tablespoons unsalted butter
10 to 12 (approximately) **shucked yearling oysters**
2 tablespoons leeks, white part only, rinsed well and sliced; slices cut in half to make ¼-inch half-moons
2 tablespoons (rounded) **fresh basil, ¼-inch slice**
1 bay leaf
1 tablespoon whole shallots, minced
2 tablespoons red bell pepper, cut into small dice
2 tablespoons Yukon Gold potatoes, peeled, cut into small dice
¼ cup champagne or sparkling wine, or Artesa Carneros Chardonnay
1 cup heavy cream
2 shakes Tabasco® Sauce
Pinch black pepper, fresh-ground
Pinch kosher or sea salt
¼ cup fresh spinach, ¼-inch slice

You can buy fresh, shucked oysters packed in a jar in most grocery stores. Select the yearling oysters, as they are the smallest size and perfect for oyster stew.

Melt the butter in a saucepan and add the oysters, leeks, basil, bay leaf, shallots, red bell pepper and potatoes. Here's the trick to perfect oyster stew: Cook the mixture slowly over medium heat, stirring often. You want to cook the oysters until they are firm—3 to 4 minutes. This will infuse the stew with the lovely nectar from the oysters, and they will be perfectly done. Once the oysters are just firm, add the champagne, heavy cream, Tabasco® Sauce, black pepper and salt. Slowly bring the stew up to just a simmer and immediately remove from the heat. Stir in the spinach at the end, just to wilt it.

Ladle the stew into bowls and add some of your favorite croutons to each bowl for crunch, or serve with some warm, crusty bread. The champagne will give the stew an effervescence and lightness. Serve the rest of the bottle with the stew.

CHEF STELLINO'S
SUGGESTED WINE PAIRING: *Voga* Pinot Grigio

Garlic-Roasted Whole Dungeness Crab & Arugula-Fennel Salad

BRIAN POOR

Serves 3 to 4

2 whole Dungeness crabs, cooked
½ cup minced fresh garlic
¼ cup minced fresh ginger
1 cube unsalted butter
½ cup minced white or yellow onion
1 teaspoon sea salt or kosher salt
¼ teaspoon red chili flakes
¼ teaspoon freshly ground black pepper
¼ cup Artesa Carneros Chardonnay
Juice of 1 lemon

FOR THE ARUGULA-FENNEL SALAD (SERVES 6 EASILY):

4 cups baby arugula (see Chef's Tips), **lightly packed**
2 cups fennel bulb, stems removed, bulbs cut in half, cores removed, shaved thin (See Chef's Tips.)
1 avocado, pit removed, cut into ½-inch slices
3 tablespoons pistachios, or any other nut you like
3 to 4 tablespoons cilantro-lime vinaigrette (see accompanying recipe), **or more to taste**

FOR THE CILANTRO-LIME VINAIGRETTE (YIELDS 3 CUPS):

1 cup honey
½ cup plus 2 tablespoons lime juice, fresh-squeezed
2 tablespoons apple cider vinegar or Pompeian® Pomegranate Infused White Balsamic Vinegar
2 tablespoons cilantro, leaves only, coarsely chopped
1 tablespoon garlic clove, minced
¼ cup fresh gingerroot, peeled and minced
½ teaspoon sea salt
¼ teaspoon black pepper, freshly ground
¼ cup Pompeian® Extra Virgin Olive Oil
¾ cup Pompeian® Extra Light Tasting Olive Oil

Preheat the oven to 425 degrees.

Hold the crab firmly with one hand and pull the shell off with your other hand. Rinse the crab under cold water into a strainer to catch the guts. Keep rinsing until you have removed most of the guts. Having some left at this point is OK.

Grasp the legs in both hands and lift up, which will snap the crab in half. You will have half of a crab in either hand. Rinse any remaining guts out.

Lay the half crabs on a firm surface and with a cleaver or heavy knife cut between the legs to separate into 10 legs and claws. Use the back side of the cleaver or knife (the non-cutting part) to smack each leg and joint gently to slightly expose the flesh of the crab. This will help the butter mixture to permeate the meat.

Place a stove-top-safe roasting pan over medium heat. Combine the garlic, ginger, butter, onion, salt, red chili flakes and black pepper in the pan and cook for 3 to 4 minutes, stirring often, until the garlic, ginger and onions are softened. Don't brown the mixture. Add the crab sections and stir well to coat all of the legs. Put into the oven and roast for about 12 to 15 minutes until the shells are lightly browned and take on a "roasty" look. Stir the garlic-butter mixture over the crab several times during the roasting process—nothing fancy; just stir the crab and the garlic-butter mixture together so the crab is well coated as it roasts. Everyone's oven cooks differently, so cooking times may vary.

When the crab is golden brown, remove, and add the Chardonnay and lemon juice to the roasting pan. Stir the mixture well and return to the oven for 4 to 5 minutes to heat the mixture through.

TO PREPARE THE ARUGULA-FENNEL SALAD:
To make the salad, simply place all the ingredients in a bowl and toss well to coat all of the leaves with the vinaigrette. You can easily adjust the amount of dressing by starting with 3 to 4 tablespoons and adding more if you like.

Serve this salad with the garlic-roasted whole Dungeness crab, and you will see how the tart, sweet notes, coupled with the complex flavors of the fennel and arugula, work fabulously well against the rich, buttery finish the crab provides.

TO PREPARE THE CILANTRO-LIME VINAIGRETTE:
Combine all the ingredients, except the two olive oils, in a blender. Turn on high and blend for about 1 minute until smooth.

Turn the blender to medium-high speed, and with the lid off, drizzle the oils slowly into the mixture. This will thicken and emulsify it.

Immediately pour the mixture into a storage container, cover, and refrigerate for 3 to 4 hours or, if possible, overnight. The dressing needs to be well chilled.

TO SERVE:
Enjoy the crab paired with arugula-fennel salad.

To serve the salad, mound it in your favorite salad bowl, pulling some avocado slices and nuts up to the top for garnish.

Return the crab to the roasting pan just before serving. To serve, place the pan on the table, and dig in. Be sure to provide a bowl to put the shells in; it'd better be a big bowl for all to share.

You can use crab crackers and picks to get at the meat as you would do for traditional cooked crab. You'll be licking your fingers over this recipe. Serve warm, crusty bread for dipping into the roasting pan juices. You'll want every bite.

CHEF'S TIPS: Baby arugula is now available ready to eat in most warehouse stores and some of your local grocery stores. With its slight bitterness and peppery finish, it's a great addition to salads.

Fennel, also called anise because of its licorice-like qualities, is available in all grocery stores. It's best shaved on an inexpensive Japanese mandoline available in most Asian markets. If one is not available, slice the fennel as thinly as you can with a sharp knife.

CHEF STELLINO'S SUGGESTED WINE PAIRING: *Codorníu Napa* Grand Reserve Sparkling Wine

Chef Poor UNSCRIPTED

WHY DO YOU DO WHAT YOU DO?
I do what I do because it is my fabric. Food is magical and ever-changing, so inspirations are constant. Besides, people love what I do, too.

WHAT IS YOUR FIRST FOOD MEMORY?
As a young kid at age 6, I ate waffles only when I went to see my grandmother "Obbie." I loved them so much, she gave me a waffle iron for Christmas. That waffle iron stayed in our family for years.

WHAT IS YOUR FAVORITE DISH TO EAT? TO PREPARE?
Has to be risotto. The slow nurturing of the ingredients resulting in a creamy yet firm bite… and the richness… Heavenly.

IS THERE A FOOD YOU HATE/DON'T LIKE?
Raw mushrooms. Taste like dirt. Love them cooked, though.

IF YOU COULD HAVE ONLY ONE FOOD FOR THE REST OF YOUR LIFE, WHAT WOULD THAT FOOD BE?
Crispy pan-fried oysters from our beach on Hood Canal in Washington state. Yummy…

WHAT OR WHO INSPIRES YOU?
My wife, Mary, inspires me. After 25 years together working in the food business, she has a great palate, understands food business trends, and isn't afraid to tell me if something I create doesn't hit the mark. Besides, she's gorgeous.

Brown Sugar-Brined, Stove Top-Smoked Wild Salmon

BRIAN POOR

Serves 4 to 5 as an appetizer

FOR THE BROWN SUGAR SMOKING BRINE (YIELDS 2 CUPS):
1¼ cups teriyaki sauce, thick and sweet, your favorite brand
½ cup water
¼ cup C&H® or Domino® Sugar
¼ cup C&H® Golden Brown Sugar or Domino® Light Brown Sugar
¼ cup Worcestershire sauce
1 tablespoon garlic cloves, minced
1 tablespoon fresh gingerroot, peeled and minced
2 tablespoons kosher or sea salt

FOR THE SALMON:
1 pound (approximately) **salmon fillet, skin on, pin bones removed**
2 cups brown sugar smoking brine
Nonstick spray (just a bit)
2 cups wood chips (I use fruit wood like cherry or apple; alder is also good.)

TO PREPARE THE BROWN SUGAR SMOKING BRINE:
Combine all of the ingredients in a heavy-bottomed saucepan over medium-high heat. Bring just to a simmer, then immediately pull off the heat and allow to cool to room temperature. Cooking the mixture will reduce moisture and could make it too thick. You just want to heat it enough to combine the flavors. Transfer to your refrigerator and chill completely.

TO PREPARE THE SALMON:
Cut the salmon into 3- to 4-inch-wide fillets and place in a nonreactive pan. Pour the brown sugar smoking brine over the salmon fillets and mix around so all of the fillets are covered well. Arrange in the pan so the fillets are well covered on all sides and not touching. Cover the fillets and place in the refrigerator overnight.

The next day, you will want to remove the fillets from the refrigerator and dry them a bit. If you have cookie cooling racks, they work best. Just remove the fillets from the brine and gently shake off the excess. You don't need to be fussy or wipe them down; the brine has done its job. Spray the rack with the nonstick spray. Lay the salmon fillets, skin side down, on the cooling racks and place back in the refrigerator for 3 to 4 hours. This allows the surface to dry, which in turn gives the finished salmon a nice look.

You will need an old, stove-top-safe roasting pan, a rack like the cookie cooling rack that will fit into the roasting pan, 4 empty small soup cans and some foil to get the smoking process going. You will also need to have a bit of an exhaust fan over your stove to remove what little smoke you will produce.

Place the soup cans in the roasting pan. Position them so they will support the rack; the cans will be the legs for the rack to sit on. The rack needs to sit lower than the top of the roasting pan so you can form a tent with the foil. Spread the wood chips evenly over the bottom of the roasting pan. Remove the now-dried salmon from the refrigerator and place it on the rack sitting on the soup cans over the wood chips in the roasting pan.

Cover the roasting pan tightly with the foil. Poke 3 pinholes in the foil to allow some venting. Place the now-ready pan on the stove over medium-high heat. When you begin to see smoke coming out of the pinholes, turn the heat down to low so there are just wisps of smoke coming out of the holes.

Continue the smoking process for 8 to 9 minutes or so, until the salmon feels firm to the touch and has a bronze look to it. You can adjust the smoking time to accommodate your desired doneness.

Remove the salmon and allow to cool.

Serve as an appetizer with the classic accompaniments of cream cheese, capers and red onion, or with spicy, savory jams and jellies. The smoked salmon can be broken up and added to cream pasta. It's also really good with scrambled eggs, or blend with cream cheese, green onions and horseradish for a great spread.

Wrap and store for up to 2 weeks in the refrigerator, or freeze for up to 3 months.

CHEF STELLINO'S SUGGESTED WINE PAIRING: *Léon Beyer* Gewürztraminer

Red & Gold Beet Salad

BRIAN POOR

Serves 2 to 3 easily

1 pound (approximately) **red and gold beets, medium size** (Leave the skin and stems on.)
¾ cup honey
1 cup rice wine vinegar
2 cups (packed) **arugula**
1 avocado, sliced into 9 to 10 slices
3 to 4 tablespoons cilantro-lime vinaigrette (See recipe on page 127.)
2 tablespoons pistachios, or any other nut you like

Rinse the beets well, place on a sheet pan, and place in a 375-degree oven. Roast the beets for about an hour until a knife easily pierces to the center. They can be overcooked, so take care to test a couple of times during the cooking process.

While the beets are cooking, whisk together the honey and rice wine vinegar in a bowl and set aside.

Remove the beets from the oven and place on the counter to cool slightly. When they are cool enough to handle but still warm, cut the stem end and root end off each and remove the skin using a paring knife. Slice the beets into 10 wedges each and place the wedges in the honey-rice wine vinegar mixture. Stir the beets well to coat.

Place the beets in the refrigerator and allow to cool completely, about 2 hours. Be sure to stir the beets a couple of times during the cooling process. As the beets cool, they will absorb the sweet-tart mixture and take on a great, complex flavor. When the beets are chilled, drain off the excess liquid.

Place the beets, arugula and avocado in a bowl. Add the cilantro-lime vinaigrette and toss well to coat all the ingredients. Arrange the salad on a platter so that it has a random look, with the beets and avocado interspersed. Scatter the pistachios over the salad.

Basil-Garlic Braised Manila Clams

BRIAN POOR

Serves 2 to 3

2 tablespoons unsalted butter
2 tablespoons fresh garlic cloves, minced
1 tablespoon whole shallots, minced
1 teaspoon fresh thyme, whole leaves
2 tablespoons (rounded) fresh basil, ¼-inch slice
2 tablespoons leeks, white part only, rinsed well and sliced; slices cut in half to make ¼-inch half-moons
Pinch red chili flakes
1 teaspoon freshly squeezed lemon juice
½ cup clam juice, bottled
1 pound medium-sized Manila clams, scrubbed and rinsed
8 or 9 strands lemon zest, for garnish

Place the butter in a saucepan with a tight-fitting lid over medium heat. When the butter has melted, add the minced garlic and shallots, fresh thyme, fresh basil, leeks and red chili flakes. Stir, and cook the mixture, uncovered, for about 1 to 1½ minutes, stirring occasionally, until the garlic, shallots and leeks have softened and the basil and thyme have become fragrant.

Add the lemon juice, clam juice and clams to the pan, and stir so the mixture is well coated. Leave the heat at medium and cover the clams with the lid. Cook for no more than 1 minute, then remove the lid.

When live clams are cooked, they seldom open all at the same time, so have your serving bowl next to the stove. As the clams just begin to pop open, remove them from the pan one by one or in groups, as the case may be. Don't wait until they have all opened before removing them, as some will be overcooked and will have become dry and tough.

Arrange the clams in the serving bowl. If you have 1 or 2 stubborn clams that appear to be refusing to open, continue to cook. They just have strong hinges. Be patient; they will give up. When all opened clams are in the bowl, pour the braising liquid over the clams and scatter the lemon zest over them to garnish. Serve with warm, crusty bread to dip in the wonderful broth.

CHEF STELLINO'S SUGGESTED WINE PAIRING: *Durbanville Hills* Sauvignon Blanc

Red & Gold Beet Salad (PREVIOUS PAGE)
Belmondo Pinot Noir

Veal Milanese
with Tomato Pesto, Salad & Shaved Parmesan

NICK STELLINO

Serves 4 to 6

2 eggs
2 tablespoons whipping cream
1½ pounds veal scaloppine
3 cups Italian-style bread crumbs
10 tablespoons Pompeian® Extra Light Tasting Olive Oil, divided

3 ounces arugula salad
Salt and pepper to taste
2 ounces shaved Parmesan pieces

FOR THE TOMATO PESTO:
3 cups tomatoes, peeled, seeded and finely diced
6 cloves garlic, finely chopped
1 teaspoon C&H® or Domino® Sugar
1 teaspoon salt
½ teaspoon dried oregano
½ teaspoon pepper
½ teaspoon onion powder
½ teaspoon red pepper flakes
2 tablespoons basil, freshly chopped
1 cup Pompeian® Extra Virgin Olive Oil

TO PREPARE THE TOMATO PESTO:
Mix all the ingredients in a bowl and let them sit undisturbed for at least an hour. All the flavors will come together as the ingredients marinate together.

TO PREPARE THE VEAL MILANESE:
In a bowl, whisk together the eggs and the cream.

Dip each of the scaloppine in the egg mixture and then the bread crumbs; make sure both sides are coated evenly. Place the scaloppine on a tray until ready to use.

Pour half the extra light tasting olive oil into a large sauté pan and cook over high heat for about 2 minutes until it starts to sizzle. Add half of the breaded scaloppine and cook over medium heat, 1 minute per side. To prevent the scaloppine from curling while you cook them, place small incisions with a sharp knife on each side of the scaloppine (along the silver skin.)

Place the cooked scaloppine on a tray lined with brown paper.

Clean the sauté pan and dispose of the oil. Cook the second batch of scaloppine in the remaining oil, following the same directions as above. Cover and keep warm.

Place the arugula in a stainless-steel bowl, and dress with 2 to 3 tablespoons of the tomato pesto. Add salt and pepper to taste.

TO SERVE:
Place the scaloppine in single-serving dishes. Top each of the scaloppine with a portion of the arugula salad and garnish with pieces of shaved Parmesan cheese. Pour some additional tomato pesto on the side of each of the scaloppine.

You should have enough for seconds.

CHEF STELLINO'S SUGGESTED WINE PAIRING: *Artesa* Estate Reserve Pinot Noir

Chef Kent Rathbun
Abacus | Dallas ~ Jasper's Restaurants | Texas

Baked-Potato Salad
Cajun Roasted Chicken Breasts with Shrimp Jambalaya Hash
Applewood-Smoked Jalapeño Shrimp
Bacon & Eggs with Niman Ranch Bacon & Duck Eggs
Dried Cherry-Chocolate Fudge Cookies

NS Chocolate Meringue Tart
Tomatoes & Bread Salad

Baked-Potato Salad

KENT RATHBUN

Makes 8 servings

2 pounds red potatoes, washed
2 ounces Pompeian® Extra Light Tasting Olive Oil
4 teaspoons kosher salt, divided
8 ounces bacon, diced
1 cup sour cream
1 bunch scallions, chopped
8 ounces sharp Cheddar cheese, grated
4 ounces whole butter, cubed
2 tablespoons cracked black pepper

In a large bowl, toss the whole red potatoes in the olive oil and 2 teaspoons kosher salt, until coated.

Place the potatoes on a sheet pan and bake at 350 degrees until they're tender.

While the potatoes are baking, cook the bacon in a small pan until crisp. Drain the excess fat and set the bacon aside.

When the potatoes are done and cool enough to work with, cut into large chunks and place in a large mixing bowl.

Add in the bacon, sour cream, scallions, sharp Cheddar cheese and butter.

Season with cracked black pepper and 2 teaspoons kosher salt. Fold all of the ingredients together, being careful to leave the potatoes chunky.

**CHEF STELLINO'S
SUGGESTED WINE PAIRING:** *Viña Zaco* Tempranillo Rioja

Cajun Roasted Chicken Breasts
with Shrimp Jambalaya Hash

KENT RATHBUN

Makes 8 servings

FOR THE CAJUN ROASTED CHICKEN BREASTS:
8 boneless, skinless chicken breasts, about 8 ounces each
¾ cup Pompeian® Extra Light Tasting Olive Oil, divided
8 cloves garlic, peeled and minced
2 jalapeño peppers, stems and seeds removed, minced
¼ cup Creole seasoning
2 tablespoons cracked black pepper
1 tablespoon kosher salt
4 lemons, juiced
1 cup Artesa Carneros Chardonnay
1 quart chicken broth
2 tablespoons fresh rosemary, chopped
¼ cup butter

FOR THE SHRIMP JAMBALAYA HASH:
½ cup Pompeian® Extra Light Tasting Olive Oil
16 shrimp (16/20 per pound), peeled and deveined, then chopped into ½-inch pieces
12 ounces andouille sausage, cut into large dice
1 cup yellow onion, cut into large dice
4 cloves garlic, peeled and minced
16 large button mushrooms, quartered
½ cup red bell pepper, seeds removed, cut into large dice
½ cup yellow bell pepper, seeds removed, cut into large dice
1 cup red potatoes, cut into large dice and blanched
1 cup sweet potatoes, cut into large dice and blanched
16 spinach leaves, julienned
12 scallions, chopped
2 tablespoons butter
1 tablespoon kosher salt
1 tablespoon cracked black pepper

TO PREPARE THE CAJUN ROASTED CHICKEN BREASTS:
Marinate the chicken breasts in ¼ cup of olive oil and the garlic, jalapeño, Creole seasoning, cracked black pepper, kosher salt and lemon juice for at least 1 hour.

In a large, hot, ovenproof sauté pan, add ½ cup of olive oil and sauté the chicken breasts until golden brown on one side. Turn the chicken breasts browned side up and add the white wine. Reduce the wine until the liquid is almost evaporated.

Add the chicken broth and transfer to a 400-degree oven. Let the chicken breasts cook for about 8 minutes.

Remove the pan from the oven and return it to the stove top. Remove the chicken from the pan and continue cooking the sauce until it starts to thicken. Finish with the chopped rosemary and the butter, and set aside.

TO PREPARE THE SHRIMP JAMBALAYA HASH:
In a large skillet, sauté the shrimp in ½ cup of olive oil until medium-rare, approximately 1 to 2 minutes.

Remove the shrimp, and set aside. Add the andouille sausage to the skillet and cook until the sausage starts to brown and release a little fat.

Add the onions and continue cooking until they start to brown. Then add the garlic, mushrooms, bell peppers and potatoes, and continue to cook for about 3 minutes.

As the vegetables start to brown, add the reserved shrimp and continue to sauté until the shrimp are done, approximately 1 to 2 minutes. Add the spinach and scallions, and finish with the butter, kosher salt and pepper.

TO SERVE:
Place the roasted chicken breasts, whole or sliced, on top of the hash, and top with sauce.

CHEF STELLINO'S SUGGESTED WINE PAIRING: *Elements by Artesa* Red Wine

Applewood-Smoked Jalapeño Shrimp (FACING PAGE)
Bodega Septima Malbec

Applewood-Smoked Jalapeño Shrimp

KENT RATHBUN

Makes 8 servings

FOR THE MARINADE:
2 ounces Pompeian® Extra Virgin Olive Oil
¼ cup red onion, peeled and chopped
1 tablespoon garlic, chopped
2 jalapeño peppers, seeded and chopped
1 bunch cilantro, chopped
4 limes, juiced
½ cup water (or beer)

FOR THE SHRIMP:
24 U-10 shrimp, peeled and deveined, then skewered (U-10 means there are under 10 per pound.)
Applewood chips, for smoking (Other types of wood chips may be used.)
2 tablespoons kosher salt

TO PREPARE THE MARINADE:
In a blender, blend all of the marinade ingredients until smooth.

TO PREPARE THE SHRIMP:
Marinate the shrimp for 45 minutes to 1 hour.

Set up a stove-top smoker with applewood chips and smoke the shrimp for 5 to 7 minutes. Season the shrimp with kosher salt and finish on a wood grill or sauté on the stove top until done. (Do not overcook; allow 5 to 7 minutes for either grilling or sautéing.)

Chef Kent Rathbun UNSCRIPTED

WHY DO YOU DO WHAT YOU DO?
What better way to make people happy than to ignite their senses with some of my culinary creations? I love to entertain, and being a chef provides me the instant gratification of knowing people are enjoying my food and having a good time doing so.

WHAT IS YOUR FIRST FOOD MEMORY?
I would have to say that my first food memory would be my mother's pan-fried chicken. The smell of that process happening across my house is unforgettable.

WHAT IS YOUR FAVORITE DISH TO EAT? TO PREPARE?
I would have to admit that I'm a carnivore...any piece of meat coming off a wood-fired grill makes me a happy boy.

IS THERE A FOOD YOU HATE/DON'T LIKE?
I am NOT a fan of chicken liver at all.

IF YOU COULD HAVE ONLY ONE FOOD FOR THE REST OF YOUR LIFE, WHAT WOULD THAT FOOD BE?
I would need an endless supply of rib-eye steaks.

WHAT OR WHO INSPIRES YOU?
Anyone who does an exceptional job of what they set out to do is someone who inspires me.

Bacon & Eggs with Niman Ranch Bacon & Duck Eggs

KENT RATHBUN

Makes 8 servings

This dish can be served anytime—not just for breakfast.

FOR THE CHIPOTLE-MOLASSES GLAZED BACON:

3 ounces canned chipotles

1 cup molasses

1 ounce whole-grain mustard

3 ounces Heinz® ketchup

3 cloves garlic, chopped

1 lime, juiced

1 teaspoon kosher salt

3 pounds Niman Ranch chipotle bacon, cut into 8 ⅜-inch-thick slices (Applewood smoked bacon may be substituted for the chipotle bacon.)

FOR THE DUCK EGGS:

8 duck eggs, cracked and set aside in a bowl

1 teaspoon kosher salt

1 tablespoon whole butter

½ ounce truffle oil

½ ounce whole black truffle, grated or chopped

2 tablespoons chives, snipped

8 slices brioche bread (our favorite type of bread), **toasted**

TO PREPARE THE CHIPOTLE-MOLASSES GLAZED BACON:

In a blender, combine the chipotles, molasses, whole-grain mustard, ketchup and garlic. Blend together until smooth.

Add the lime juice and kosher salt. Strain through a fine-mesh chinois.

Grill the bacon slices on both sides until rendered and crispy. Brush the bacon with the chipotle-molasses glaze before serving. Reserve the remaining glaze.

TO PREPARE THE DUCK EGGS:

In a mixing bowl, whisk the duck eggs and kosher salt until smooth.

In a sauté pan, combine the whole butter and truffle oil, and set on medium heat.

When the whole butter is melted, add the duck egg mixture and scramble the eggs. Keep them soft.

Garnish the cooked eggs with the black truffle and the chives. Reserve a small portion of the truffle and chives for service.

TO SERVE:

Using a pastry brush, make a brushstroke on a plate with some of the reserved chipotle-molasses glaze. Place a slice of toasted brioche bread on the plate. Place a spoonful of scrambled eggs on top of the brioche toast. Garnish with the reserved truffle and chives.

Place the chipotle bacon on the side of the plate and drizzle chipotle-molasses glaze on top.

CHEF STELLINO'S SUGGESTED WINE PAIRING: *Two Oceans* Sauvignon Blanc

"Sometimes, when we pay attention, we realize the immensity of the beauty that surrounds us, reflected in the most common things, as if hiding in plain sight..."

Dried Cherry-Chocolate Fudge Cookies

KENT RATHBUN

Yields 60 2-bite cookies

¾ cup dried cherries
¼ cup amaretto
1½ cups bittersweet chocolate
3 ounces butter
2¼ cups C&H® Golden Brown Sugar or Domino® Light Brown Sugar
1 teaspoon baking powder
2 eggs
1 egg yolk
2 teaspoons vanilla extract
⅔ cup all-purpose flour
1¼ cups semisweet chocolate chips

Pour the amaretto over the dried cherries and allow them to sit until most of the liquid is absorbed.

Melt the bittersweet chocolate and butter, and set aside to cool.

Combine the brown sugar, baking powder, whole eggs, egg yolk and vanilla. Add to the cherries. Stir in the melted chocolate mixture, the flour and the semisweet chips, and stir until well combined.

Place the batter in the refrigerator to cool for about 30 minutes.

Scoop out rounded tablespoon-size scoops onto a sheet pan that is lined with parchment paper or a silicone mat. Bake at 350 degrees for 10 to 14 minutes.

Allow the cookies to cool on the baking sheet for 5 to 10 minutes before moving them; they will be very soft. Serve.

CHEF STELLINO'S SUGGESTED WINE PAIRING: *Codorníu* Sparkling Pinot Noir

Chocolate Meringue Tart

NICK STELLINO

Makes 1 11-inch tart

Sweet shortcrust pastry (See accompanying recipe.)
Chocolate cream filling (See accompanying recipe.)
6 ounces semisweet chocolate, chopped
¼ cup rum or crème de cacao (optional)

FOR THE SHORTCRUST PASTRY:
1½ cups all-purpose flour, plus extra for dusting the work surface
½ teaspoon C&H® or Domino® Sugar
¼ teaspoon salt
1 cup chilled butter, cut into ½-inch dice
1 egg, lightly beaten
4 tablespoons cold water

FOR THE CHOCOLATE CREAM FILLING (YIELDS 2¾ CUPS):
2 cups half-and-half
1 teaspoon vanilla extract
6 ounces semisweet chocolate, chopped into small pieces
1 cup C&H® or Domino® Sugar
¼ cup all-purpose flour
⅛ teaspoon salt
6 large egg yolks

FOR THE MERINGUE TOPPING:
1 tablespoon cornstarch
1 tablespoon cold water
½ cup boiling water
3 egg whites
8 tablespoons C&H® or Domino® Sugar
1 teaspoon vanilla extract

TO PREPARE THE SHORTCRUST PASTRY:
Preheat the oven to 375 degrees.

In a food processor, combine the flour, sugar and salt with 1 pulse. Add all of the butter, and pulse until the mixture is crumbly. Add the egg and cold water, and pulse just until moistened. Turn the dough out onto a flat surface and form it into a ball. Flatten the ball and wrap in plastic. Chill for at least 30 minutes.

Turn the dough out onto a lightly floured surface and roll it into a 12-inch circle. Place into an 11-inch tart pan with a removable bottom, and trim off the excess. Prick the pie pastry with a fork.

Line the inside of the pastry shell with foil and fill with dried beans. Bake in the oven for 20 minutes, until the edges are golden brown. Remove the foil and beans, and bake the shell for 5 more minutes. Take it out of the oven and let it cool.

TO PREPARE THE CHOCOLATE CREAM FILLING:

Heat the half-and-half in a nonreactive saucepan over medium heat. Add the vanilla extract and chocolate. Stir well until all the chocolate has melted. Stir together the sugar, flour and salt in a mixing bowl. Whisk in the egg yolks. Continue to whisk until well blended. The color of the mixture will lighten slightly.

Slowly, in a thin stream, pour a third of the hot half-and-half into the egg mixture. Whisk well as you are pouring, both to incorporate the egg and to avoid cooking it.

Pour the warm egg mixture into the saucepan with the remaining half-and-half. Whisk immediately and well.

Cook over medium heat, whisking constantly, until the mixture reaches a thick, creamy consistency, about 6 to 8 minutes.

Pour the chocolate cream from the hot saucepan through a strainer into a clean bowl; this will give you a smoother filling. If you are going to bake the tart right away, pour the chocolate cream filling into the prebaked and cooled pie shell, spreading it so that the top is smooth. Alternatively, you can make the chocolate cream filling ahead and store it in the refrigerator, covered, for up to 3 days. Before refrigerating, cover the surface of the filling with a piece of plastic film wrap in order to prevent the cream from developing a skin.

TO PREPARE THE MERINGUE TOPPING:

Mix the cornstarch and cold water well. Add boiling water. Stir well until thick, pour through a small strainer into a bowl, then cool in the refrigerator until cold.

Beat the egg whites to soft peaks. Add sugar 1 tablespoon at a time. Add the cooled cornstarch. Continue beating until stiff, then add the vanilla extract.

Spread the meringue topping on the pie; bake at 375 degrees for 15 minutes, or until brown. Turn off the heat and let cool in the oven with the oven door open.

CHEF STELLINO'S SUGGESTED WINE PAIRING: *Artesa* Artisan Series Orange Muscat

Tomatoes & Bread Salad

NICK STELLINO

Serves 4

1 recipe homemade Parmesan-glazed croutons (See accompanying recipe.)
10 ounces cherry tomatoes, cut in half
½ red onion, thinly sliced and marinated in 1 cup chilled water and 2 tablespoons Pompeian® Pomegranate Infused White Balsamic Vinegar for at least 30 minutes, then drained
1 recipe tomato dressing with feta cheese (See accompanying recipe.)
5 ounces baby arugula
1 tablespoon drained capers
4 tablespoons crumbled feta cheese

FOR THE PARMESAN-GLAZED CROUTONS:
2 cups day-old bread, cut into ½-inch cubes
2 tablespoons grated Parmesan cheese, divided
½ teaspoon dried oregano
½ teaspoon garlic powder
½ teaspoon onion powder
½ teaspoon paprika
½ teaspoon pepper
4 tablespoons Pompeian® Extra Virgin Olive Oil

FOR THE TOMATO DRESSING WITH FETA CHEESE:
2 ounces cherry tomatoes
2 tablespoons crumbled feta cheese
1 tablespoon shallots, chopped
1 tablespoon basil, chopped
3 teaspoons C&H® or Domino® Organic Agave Nectar, or 1 teaspoon C&H® or Domino® Sugar
1½ tablespoons Pompeian® Red Wine Vinegar
½ teaspoon salt
5 tablespoons Pompeian® Extra Virgin Olive Oil

TO PREPARE THE PARMESAN-GLAZED CROUTONS:
Preheat the oven to 200 degrees.

Mix all the ingredients, using 1 tablespoon of the Parmesan for this step and reserving the remaining tablespoon. Be sure to coat the croutons well.

Place the croutons on a baking tray and bake in the oven for 1 hour. Turn off the heat, pour the croutons into a bowl, and mix with the remaining Parmesan.

Place the croutons back on the tray and let them rest in the warm oven for 1 more hour. Now they are ready to be served.

TO PREPARE THE TOMATO DRESSING WITH FETA CHEESE:
Place all the ingredients into a food processor and process for 1 to 2 minutes, until they are all amalgamated together into a delicious salad dressing.

TO ASSEMBLE THE SALAD:
Mix the croutons, tomatoes and onion with half of the dressing and let the mixture rest for 15 to 20 minutes.

Add the arugula, capers and feta, plus half of the remaining dressing. Dress the salad, serve, and drizzle each plate with the remaining dressing.

CHEF STELLINO'S SUGGESTED WINE PAIRING: *Elements by Artesa* Red Wine

Chef Kevin Rathbun
Rathbun's | Atlanta

YaYa's Eggplant Fries with Confectioners Sugar
Pan-Roasted Wahoo with Eggplant Caviar & Local Tomato-Basil Salad
Cauliflower & Parmesan Soup with Cured-Olive Crostini
Brown-Sugared Pork Belly, Creamed Cabbage & Mustard Greens
Sea Scallop Benedict with Country Ham Grits & Tabasco Hollandaise
Gooey Toffee Cakes with Toasted-Pecan Ice Cream

NS Asparagus Soup with a
Confit of Peppers & Asparagus Tips

YaYa's Eggplant Fries with Confectioners Sugar

KEVIN RATHBUN

Makes 4 servings

½ teaspoon salt (fine)
¾ cup all-purpose flour
1 eggplant
1 cup milk
3 whole eggs
2 cups Progresso® Italian-style bread crumbs
4 cups Pompeian® Extra Light Tasting Olive Oil, for frying
4 tablespoons C&H® Powdered Sugar or Domino® Confectioners Sugar, divided
2 tablespoons Tabasco® Sauce

Mix the salt with the flour. Cut the eggplant into pieces (each should be about 2 inches long and ½ inch thick), and place into the flour. In a mixing bowl, combine the milk and eggs, and whisk.

Place the flour-coated eggplant slices into the egg wash and then coat them in the bread crumbs. In a small frying pot, heat the oil to 350 degrees and fry the breaded eggplant pieces until golden brown. Transfer the eggplant fries to a plate lined with paper towels and drain the excess oil.

Transfer the fries to another plate and generously coat with 2 tablespoons powdered/confectioners sugar. In a small bowl, mix the remaining 2 tablespoons powdered/confectioners sugar with the Tabasco® Sauce. Serve this sauce on the side in a ramekin.

CHEF STELLINO'S SUGGESTED WINE PAIRING: *Voga* Sparkling Pinot Grigio

Pan-Roasted Wahoo with Eggplant Caviar & Local Tomato-Basil Salad

KEVIN RATHBUN

Makes 4 servings

1 pound wahoo loin
1 tablespoon chipotle chili powder
2 teaspoons kosher salt
1 tablespoon Pompeian® Extra Light Tasting Olive Oil

FOR THE MARINADE:

½ cup white wine vinegar or Pompeian® Pomegranate Infused White Balsamic Vinegar
2 tablespoons lime juice
¼ cup orange juice
¼ cup Pompeian® Extra Virgin Olive Oil
½ cup cilantro, chopped
3 teaspoons kosher salt
1 teaspoon black pepper

FOR THE EGGPLANT CAVIAR:

1 large eggplant, split in half
1 tablespoon plus ¼ cup Pompeian® Extra Virgin Olive Oil
2 teaspoons kosher salt
1 teaspoon black pepper
1 tablespoon C&H® or Domino® Sugar
2 teaspoons thyme, chopped
3 tablespoons seasoned bread crumbs

FOR THE TOMATO-BASIL SALAD:

1 cup assorted heirloom tomatoes, cut into ½-inch dice
¼ cup red onion, thinly sliced
¼ cup basil leaves, torn
3 tablespoons Pompeian® Red Wine Vinegar
¼ cup Pompeian® Extra Virgin Olive Oil
2 teaspoons kosher salt
½ teaspoon black pepper

TO PREPARE THE WAHOO:
Generously season the wahoo loin with the chili powder and salt.

In a sauté pan, heat the olive oil to the smoking point and sear the wahoo loin on both sides to color it. (The fish should remain rare.) After searing the wahoo loin, place it in the refrigerator in the marinade for up to 2 hours.

TO PREPARE THE MARINADE:
In a small bowl, mix the vinegar, lime and orange juice, olive oil, cilantro, salt and pepper.

TO PREPARE THE EGGPLANT CAVIAR:
Preheat the oven to 400 degrees.

Coat the eggplant halves with 1 tablespoon extra virgin olive oil, and season with salt and pepper. Place cut side down on a cookie sheet lined with parchment pepper. Place the eggplant in the oven for 30 to 40 minutes, or until it's completely soft.

Remove the eggplant from the oven and chop and mash it into a paste. Transfer to a bowl and mix in ¼ cup extra virgin olive oil, sugar, thyme and seasoned bread crumbs. Reserve.

TO PREPARE THE TOMATO-BASIL SALAD:
In a small bowl, mix the tomatoes, red onion, basil, vinegar, extra virgin olive oil, salt and pepper. Let marinate for 5 minutes.

TO SERVE:
For plating, heat the fish in its marinade to 110 degrees so that it's just warm. Place one-fourth of the eggplant caviar in the center of the plate. Slice the wahoo ¼ inch thick, and place 3 to 4 slices on top of the caviar. Top with tomato-basil salad, and enjoy.

CHEF STELLINO'S SUGGESTED WINE PAIRING: *Terras Gauda* Abadía de San Campio Albariño

Cauliflower & Parmesan Soup with Cured-Olive Crostini

KEVIN RATHBUN

Makes 6 servings

FOR THE SOUP:
1 head cauliflower, chunked
2 shallots, chopped
1½ cups heavy whipping cream
1½ cups chicken broth
¾ cup Parmesan cheese
2 tablespoons lemon juice
2 tablespoons honey
1 tablespoon kosher salt
½ tablespoon black pepper
Pompeian® Extra Virgin Olive Oil, for drizzling over the soup

FOR THE CROSTINI:
6 French-bread rounds
Pompeian® Extra Virgin Olive Oil
6 piquillo peppers (roasted Spanish red peppers)

FOR THE GARNISH:
¼ cup cured olives, chopped
1 tablespoon micro basil
3 teaspoons Pompeian® Extra Virgin Olive Oil
1 teaspoon lemon juice

TO PREPARE THE SOUP:
Place the cauliflower, shallots, cream and broth in a small pot and bring to a boil. Slow to a simmer and cook until the cauliflower is tender. Transfer to a blender and puree until smooth. While the soup is blending, add the Parmesan, processing until smooth.

To finish, add the lemon juice, honey, salt and pepper. Serve hot.

TO PREPARE THE CROSTINI:
Brush the French-bread rounds with olive oil, and toast in the oven at 350 degrees for 8 to 10 minutes. Place 1 piquillo pepper on each round. Garnish the toasted rounds with chopped olives, micro basil, olive oil and a little lemon juice.

Place the hot soup in a bowl and float a crostini on top. Drizzle extra virgin olive oil over the soup.

CHEF STELLINO'S SUGGESTED WINE PAIRING: *Elements by Artesa* Chardonnay

Chef Kevin Rathbun UNSCRIPTED

WHY DO YOU DO WHAT YOU DO?

I have only known the restaurant business. I started young and was encouraged by many great chefs to take it to a higher level. My passion for making people happy is instant gratification; therefore, it is easy to love what I do.

WHAT IS YOUR FIRST FOOD MEMORY?

My mother's fried chicken and my grandmother's homemade noodles come to mind. Being from Kansas City and growing up with BBQ is a great memory as well.

WHAT IS YOUR FAVORITE DISH TO EAT? TO PREPARE?

Favorite dish...I am a sucker for great steak and potatoes, but for comfort, homemade biscuits and sausage gravy. Oh, yeah, it's a Midwest thing.

IS THERE A FOOD YOU HATE/DON'T LIKE?

I love all sorts of foods. Don't have any hates, although cod sperm was very unusual, and I'll probably pass on the offering next time. Durian fruit stinks so bad that I can't stomach the fact of trying to eat it.

IF YOU COULD HAVE ONLY ONE FOOD FOR THE REST OF YOUR LIFE, WHAT WOULD THAT FOOD BE?

Great bread would be very hard to do without, pasta a secondary.

WHAT OR WHO INSPIRES YOU?

I am inspired by motivated people, people who energize others and teach with a passion, great magazines and cookbooks of all kinds, and mostly my staff; they are the nuts and bolts of our restaurants.

Brown-Sugared Pork Belly, Creamed Cabbage & Mustard Greens

KEVIN RATHBUN

Makes 6 servings

FOR THE PORK BELLY:
2 pounds pork belly
2 tablespoons kosher salt
½ tablespoon black pepper
1 cup C&H® Golden Brown Sugar or Domino® Light Brown Sugar
¼ cup Pompeian® Red Wine Vinegar
½ tablespoon red chili flakes

FOR THE CREAMED CABBAGE:
4 cups white cabbage, chopped
Ice water
1 cup heavy cream
1 tablespoon garlic, minced
Kosher salt to taste
½ teaspoon black pepper
1 tablespoon cornstarch
1 tablespoon water
1 cup mustard greens, chiffonade

FOR THE GARNISH:
1 cup celery leaves

TO PREPARE THE PORK BELLY:
Preheat the oven to 300 degrees.

Score the pork belly and season with salt and pepper. In a small bowl, combine the brown sugar, vinegar and red chili flakes. Brush the pork belly generously with the brown sugar mixture. Place in the oven and roast for 2½ hours.

Remove from the oven and let rest.

TO PREPARE THE CABBAGE:

In a large pot, add 2 quarts of water. Bring to a boil and blanch the cabbage for 5 minutes. Strain, and shock in ice water to slow the cooking process. Strain again, and reserve.

In a small pot, combine the cream and garlic. Reduce by half and season with salt and pepper. Mix 1 tablespoon cornstarch and 1 tablespoon water together, and then add to the cream-and-garlic mixture. Simmer for 5 minutes, then add the drained cabbage to the cream and stir in the mustard greens.

Divide the creamed cabbage and pork belly into 6 equal portions. Place the cabbage in the center of each plate, and top with the pork belly. Garnish with the celery leaves, and serve.

CHEF STELLINO'S SUGGESTED WINE PAIRING: *Scala Dei* Prior

Sea Scallop Benedict with Country Ham Grits & Tabasco Hollandaise

KEVIN RATHBUN

Makes 6 servings

FOR THE COUNTRY HAM GRITS:
1 tablespoon Pompeian® Extra Light Tasting Olive Oil
¾ cup country ham, cut into ¼-inch dice
2 tablespoons shallots, minced
1 cup stone-ground grits
4 cups chicken stock
1 teaspoon black pepper
½ cup heavy cream

FOR THE HOLLANDAISE:
4 large egg yolks
1 tablespoon lemon juice
10 dashes Tabasco® Sauce
1 cup warm clarified butter
2 teaspoons salt

FOR THE SCALLOPS:
3 tablespoons Pompeian® Extra Light Tasting Olive Oil
18 U-10 dry pack sea scallops (U-10 is fewer than 10 to a pound.)
1 tablespoon kosher salt
2 teaspoons black pepper

FOR THE GARNISH:
¼ cup chives, minced

TO PREPARE THE COUNTRY HAM GRITS:
In a preheated small, heavy-bottomed pot, add the oil, ham and shallots. Sauté for 5 minutes until the ham is cooked through, then add the grits, stock and pepper. Simmer for 30 minutes. Add the cream and continue to cook for 10 minutes, stirring constantly. Reserve.

TO PREPARE THE HOLLANDAISE:
Bring water to a simmer in the lower portion of a small double boiler. Place the yolks, lemon juice and Tabasco® Sauce in a stainless-steel bowl and place over the simmering water. Whisking vigorously, start adding warm butter, a little at a time. If the mixture starts to thicken too much, add a little hot water to thin it. Continue to add butter until the mixture coats the back of a spoon. Season with salt, and reserve.

TO PREPARE THE SCALLOPS:
Add the oil to a hot sauté pan. Season the scallops on both sides, then sear them on both sides until golden brown, approximately 2 minutes per side.

TO SERVE:
For plating, place 2 tablespoons of hot grits in the center of the plate. Surround the grits with 3 scallops, and drizzle with hollandaise. Garnish with chives, and enjoy.

CHEF STELLINO'S SUGGESTED WINE PAIRING: *Bodega Septima* Chardonnay

Gooey Toffee Cakes with Toasted-Pecan Ice Cream

KEVIN RATHBUN

Makes 12 servings

FOR THE TOFFEE CAKES:
6 ounces dates, pitted
1¼ cups water
1 teaspoon baking soda
1½ cups all-purpose flour
1 teaspoon baking powder
4 ounces butter
¾ cup C&H® or Domino® Sugar
2 eggs
1 teaspoon vanilla extract

FOR THE TOFFEE SAUCE:
2½ cups C&H® Golden Brown Sugar or Domino® Light Brown Sugar
3½ ounces butter
1 cup half-and-half
½ ounce brandy
1 teaspoon vanilla extract
6 ounces Heath® bar bits

FOR THE TOASTED-PECAN ICE CREAM:
3 cups milk
1 cinnamon stick
½ vanilla bean, split and scraped, bean discarded
1½ cups pecan pieces
Ice, for an ice bath
1 cup C&H® or Domino® Sugar, divided
6 egg yolks
½ teaspoon whiskey

TO PREPARE THE TOFFEE CAKES:

Preheat the oven to 325 degrees and spray 12 4-ounce aluminum cups with nonstick cooking spray.

Combine the dates and water in a saucepan and bring to a boil. Turn off the heat and gradually add the baking soda (it will foam) and set aside.

Sift together the flour and baking powder. Cream the butter and the sugar together in a mixer bowl until fluffy. With the mixer running, add the eggs and mix until incorporated. Add the vanilla, and continue to mix until smooth. To the creamed mixture, add the flour mixture in thirds, alternating with the dates; continue to stir until all is well combined and smooth.

Place equal amounts of the mixture into the prepared aluminum cups and bake for 40 minutes, or until a toothpick inserted comes out clean.

TO PREPARE THE TOFFEE SAUCE:
Combine the sugar, butter, half-and-half and brandy; boil for 3 minutes. Add the vanilla and Heath® bar bits, and stir until almost smooth.

Preheat the oven to 400 degrees.

While the sauce is warm, ladle equal amounts of it onto the cooked cakes and cook for 5 more minutes, or until bubbly and golden. Let cool to room temperature.

TO PREPARE THE TOASTED-PECAN ICE CREAM:
Preheat the oven to 350 degrees.

In a saucepan, bring the milk, cinnamon stick and vanilla to a boil. While the mixture is coming to a boil, toast the pecan pieces in the oven for 6 to 8 minutes. Toss them into the milk mixture. Turn off the heat and let the milk mixture rest for at least 10 minutes.

While the milk is resting, prepare an ice bath with a strainer. (Place 1 small bowl into a large bowl of ice.) Bring the milk back to a boil with half of the sugar. Whisk the other half of the sugar into the egg yolks until lemony in color.

When the milk comes to a boil, create a liaison, or thickening agent, by pouring the hot milk, a bit at a time, into the yolks and stirring (being careful not to overcook the yolks); then pour the mixture back into the saucepan with the heat on low. Cook until slightly thick (2 to 3 minutes), stirring with a spatula so as not to create air bubbles. Pour through the strainer into the ice bath to cool the mixture down rapidly. Add the whiskey. Let cool, then place in an ice-cream machine and process to the manufacturer's specifications.

Serve the toffee cakes accompanied by the toasted-pecan ice cream.

Asparagus Soup with a Confit of Peppers & Asparagus Tips

NICK STELLINO

Serves 4

4 tablespoons Pompeian® Extra Light Tasting Olive Oil
1 white onion, chopped
2 celery stalks, chopped
8 garlic cloves, thickly sliced
2 medium carrots, peeled and cut into ½-inch rounds
½ teaspoon dried thyme
½ teaspoon red pepper flakes
2 pounds asparagus (Peel the spears and cut into ½-inch slices; set the tips aside, reserving half for the confit.)
½ cup sherry
6 cups chicken broth
¾ cup sour cream, for garnish
6 small sprigs fresh dill, cut into small pieces, for garnish

1 recipe Confit of Peppers & Asparagus Tips (See recipe on page 172.)

In a stockpot, heat the extra light tasting olive oil over high heat. Add the onion, celery, garlic, carrots, thyme and red pepper flakes to the pot. Cook over medium-high heat, stirring well, until the onions begin to soften, about 3 to 4 minutes. Add the asparagus pieces and half of the tips.

Add the sherry, bring to a boil, and stir well to dislodge the brown bits at the bottom of the pot. Cook until the sherry is reduced by half, about 3 minutes. Add the chicken broth and bring to a boil; reduce the heat to medium-low and cook for 40 to 45 minutes, stirring well every 15 minutes. Add the soup, in batches, to a food processor and process it to a smooth, cream-like consistency. Strain, place the soup back in the stockpot, and keep warm.

Serve the soup in bowls and garnish with sour cream and fresh dill. Decorate with the Confit of Peppers & Asparagus Tips.

CHEF STELLINO'S SUGGESTED WINE PAIRING: *Artesa* Carneros Pinot Noir

Confit of Peppers & Asparagus Tips

NICK STELLINO

Serves 4

2 tablespoons Pompeian® Extra Virgin Olive Oil
1 shallot, finely diced
1 small red bell pepper, finely diced
1 small yellow bell pepper, finely diced
1 cup asparagus tips, cut in half
2 garlic cloves, finely chopped
¼ teaspoon red pepper flakes
2 tablespoons brandy
2 tablespoons softened butter
Salt and pepper to taste
½ teaspoon truffle oil (optional, for an extra kick)

Cook the olive oil over high heat until it sizzles, then lower the heat to medium-low. Add the shallot, stir well, and cook for 2 minutes, then add the peppers and the asparagus, and mix together. Increase the heat to medium-high and cook, stirring well, for 2 more minutes.

Add the garlic and the red pepper flakes, and stir well for 1 minute. Then add the brandy and cook 1 more minute.

Reduce the heat to medium-low, add the butter, and stir well until completely melted. Add salt and pepper to taste. Add the optional truffle oil, stirring well before serving.

Set aside and keep warm until ready to use.

"Hello," he said. "He looks so handsome!" she thought. They fell in love, and together they made a delightful soup.

Every dish has a story.

Chef John Tesar
The Tesar Restaurant Group | Dallas

Olive Oil-Poached White Anchovies & Squid-Ink Spaghetti, Sicilian Style

Lime & Curry-Marinated Grass-Fed Rib-Eye Steaks with Cucumber & Honeydew Melon Chutney & Spiced Basmati Rice

Fig & Pepper Cress Salad with Goat's Milk Yogurt, Goat Cheese, & Meyer Lemon & Honey Vinaigrette

Rhubarb Parfait

NS Steak & Salad with a Balsamic-Parmesan Dressing

Easy Chocolate Mousse

Olive Oil-Poached White Anchovies & Squid-Ink Spaghetti, Sicilian Style

JOHN TESAR

Serves 4

1 large fennel bulb (Reserve any fronds for garnish.)
⅛ teaspoon crumbled saffron threads
½ cup golden raisins
½ cup Artesa Carneros Chardonnay
1 medium onion, finely chopped
1 tablespoon fennel seeds, crushed
½ cup Pompeian® Extra Virgin Olive Oil
Salt to taste
12 ounces olive oil-poached white anchovies, divided
1 pound squid-ink spaghetti or DaVinci® spaghetti
½ cup pine nuts, toasted
Pepper to taste
⅓ cup dry bread crumbs, toasted and tossed with 2 tablespoons Pompeian® Extra Virgin Olive Oil and salt to taste

Finely chop the fennel bulb. Combine the saffron, raisins and wine in a bowl. Cook the onion, chopped fennel and fennel seeds in the olive oil with salt to taste in a 12-inch heavy skillet over moderate heat, stirring, until the fennel is tender, about 15 minutes.

Add the wine mixture and half of the anchovies, breaking the anchovies up with a fork; simmer 1 minute. Remove the sauce from the heat and let the flavors infuse.

Cook the pasta in a 6- to 8-quart pot of boiling salted water until al dente, and then drain in a colander. Add the pasta to the fennel sauce. If necessary, warm the sauce up again; remove from the heat when you are ready to add the rest of the ingredients.

To finish, add the remaining anchovies, the reserved fennel fronds, the pine nuts, and salt and pepper to taste. Add the bread crumbs and toss again.

CHEF STELLINO'S SUGGESTED WINE PAIRING: *Ca'Montini* Pinot Grigio

Lime & Curry-Marinated Grass-Fed Rib-Eye Steaks
with Cucumber & Honeydew Melon Chutney & Spiced Basmati Rice

JOHN TESAR

Serves 4

FOR THE CHUTNEY:
2 cups chopped firm-ripe honeydew melon (10 ounces)
⅓ seedless cucumber, peeled and chopped (about ¾ cup)
½ cup chopped red onion
3 tablespoons fresh lime juice
¼ cup chopped cilantro
¼ cup fresh mint
1 to 2 teaspoons minced fresh jalapeño, seeds removed
¼ teaspoon salt
½ teaspoon ground coriander
¼ teaspoon ground cumin

FOR THE STEAK:
2 tablespoons fresh lime juice
1 tablespoon Pompeian® Extra Light Tasting Olive Oil
1 tablespoon green Madras curry powder
2 teaspoons salt
1 teaspoon pepper
2 14-ounce grass-fed rib-eye steaks

FOR THE SPICED BASMATI RICE (SERVES 6 TO 8):
2 cups white basmati rice
3½ cups chicken broth (28 fluid ounces)
1 3-inch cinnamon stick
4 Turkish bay leaves
1 tablespoon unsalted butter

Fresh mint and cilantro, for garnish

TO PREPARE THE CHUTNEY:
Stir together the honeydew, cucumber, onion, lime juice, cilantro, mint, jalapeño and ¼ teaspoon salt. Season with the coriander and cumin, and let the chutney stand while grilling the steak.

TO PREPARE THE STEAK:

Prepare a gas grill for direct-heat cooking over medium heat. (I prefer a hardwood charcoal grill.)

Stir together the lime juice, oil, curry powder, 2 teaspoons salt and 1 teaspoon pepper. Coat the steak with the curry mixture.

Oil the grill rack, then grill the steak, covered. Cook for 9 minutes total for medium-rare.

Let the steak rest on a cutting board for 5 minutes, and then slice thinly across the grain. Serve the steak with the chutney and jasmine or spiced basmati rice (see accompanying recipe), and garnish with fresh mint and cilantro.

TO PREPARE THE SPICED BASMATI RICE:

Rinse the rice in several changes of cold water until the water runs clear. Drain well in a sieve. Bring the rice, broth, cinnamon stick and bay leaves to a boil in a 4-quart heavy pot over high heat. Reduce the heat to low and cook, covered, until the rice is tender and the liquid is absorbed, about 15 minutes. Remove from the heat and let stand, covered and undisturbed, for 5 minutes. Discard the bay leaves, then stir in the butter until melted. Fluff gently with a fork.

CHEF STELLINO'S SUGGESTED WINE PAIRING: *Elements by Artesa* Merlot

Fig & Pepper Cress Salad
with Goat's Milk Yogurt, Goat Cheese, & Meyer Lemon & Honey Vinaigrette

JOHN TESAR

Serves 4

FOR THE VINAIGRETTE:
½ cup goat's milk yogurt
½ cup soft fresh goat cheese, crumbled
2 teaspoons clover honey
½ teaspoon (scant) vanilla extract
2 tablespoons fresh Meyer lemon juice
Kosher salt to taste

FOR THE SALAD:
24 ripe black Mission figs, halved lengthwise
Maldon sea salt
2 bunches pepper cress or watercress, thick stems trimmed (about 3 cups)
1 cup (loosely packed) small mint leaves
Pompeian® Extra Virgin Olive Oil
Grains of paradise

TO PREPARE THE VINAIGRETTE:
Whisk together the first 5 ingredients in a medium bowl. Season with salt, and reserve.

TO PREPARE THE SALAD:
Sprinkle the figs with Maldon salt and set in the center of the plate. Drizzle the vinaigrette on the figs; scatter pepper cress and mint over them. Finish by drizzling with olive oil and seasoning with grains of paradise.

CHEF STELLINO'S SUGGESTED WINE PAIRING: *Legaris* Verdejo

Chef Tesar UNSCRIPTED

WHY DO YOU DO WHAT YOU DO?
I cook because I love it—the energy, the passion, the artistic expression. I also love to teach, meet new and interesting people, and find and cook with some of the most amazing ingredients on the planet. I am truly blessed.

WHAT IS YOUR FIRST FOOD MEMORY?
My mother cooking in our kitchen at home every day, all day. But everything was fresh, local and made with love, breakfast, lunch and dinner.

WHAT IS YOUR FAVORITE DISH TO EAT? TO PREPARE?
My favorite dish to eat is still an amazing fresh piece of fish or shellfish right out of the water. I love to cook with fresh fish and fresh produce no matter what they are. I like to challenge myself to create new items and combinations all the time.

IS THERE A FOOD YOU HATE/DON'T LIKE?
Anything from a can or box, or frozen.

IF YOU COULD HAVE ONLY ONE FOOD FOR THE REST OF YOUR LIFE, WHAT WOULD THAT FOOD BE?
Caviar, so I can eat it with my champagne.

WHAT OR WHO INSPIRES YOU?
Many chefs inspire me, but I would have to say Eric Ripert, for his understanding of freshness, simplicity and precise execution, and Rick Moonen, for his energy and all the opportunities working for him has provided me. Nick Stellino, for his charm, kindness and intelligent manner.

Rhubarb Parfait

JOHN TESAR

Serves 6

1½ pounds fresh, ripe rhubarb, trimmed and sliced ½ inch thick (about 4 cups or 1 pound prepped)
½ cup honey
Zest and juice of 1 orange
½ teaspoon lemon juice
2 tablespoons finely chopped candied ginger
½ Tahitian vanilla bean, split
Pinch Maldon sea salt
¾ cup heavy whipping cream
2 tablespoons C&H® or Domino® Sugar

FOR CANDIED RHUBARB STRIPS (OPTIONAL):
1 stalk rhubarb
½ cup (3½ ounces) C&H® or Domino® Sugar
1 cup water

If you would like to garnish the dessert with candied rhubarb strips, make them first.

TO PREPARE THE PARFAIT:
Put the rhubarb, honey, orange zest and orange and lemon juices, candied ginger, vanilla bean and Maldon salt in a saucepan over medium heat. Stir to combine. Then cover and cook, stirring every few minutes, for 10 minutes, until the mixture has come to a boil and the rhubarb has softened. Remove from the heat and allow to cool. Remove the vanilla bean and transfer the compote to a bowl. Refrigerate, uncovered, for at least 30 minutes, until very cold.

Whip the cream and sugar—either by hand or using an electric mixer—until soft peaks form; the mixture should be stiff but not grainy. Set aside ⅓ cup of the compote to garnish the dessert, then fold the remaining compote into the whipped cream. Spoon the fool into 6 ½-cup glasses or dishes, and chill for 1 hour before serving topped with the reserved compote. Candied rhubarb strips (see accompanying recipe) may be added as an optional garnish.

TO PREPARE CANDIED RHUBARB STRIPS:
Preheat the oven to 200 degrees. Line a baking sheet with a Silpat® mat or lightly greased parchment.

Cut the rhubarb into 6-inch lengths. Cut each piece into strips ⅛ inch thick with a good peeler or mandoline. Combine the sugar and water in a saucepan over high heat and bring to a boil. Cook and stir until the sugar is dissolved, then remove from the heat. Dip the rhubarb ribbons into the syrup, then place them on the prepared baking sheet, laying them out flat and ensuring that they do not touch each other. Bake for about 45 minutes, until dry.

CHEF STELLINO'S SUGGESTED WINE PAIRING: *Anna de Codorníu* Brut Rosé

Steak & Salad with a Balsamic-Parmesan Dressing

NICK STELLINO

Serves 4

2 1-pound steaks (New York or rib-eye), **each 1½ inches thick**
Salt and freshly ground pepper to taste
2 tablespoons Pompeian® Extra Virgin Olive Oil
5 ounces baby arugula salad
Balsamic-Parmesan dressing (See accompanying recipe.)
2 ounces shaved Parmesan

FOR THE BALSAMIC-PARMESAN DRESSING:
½ cup Pompeian® Balsamic Vinegar
4 tablespoons shallots, finely chopped
2 garlic cloves, finely chopped
1 cup Pompeian® Extra Virgin Olive Oil
8 tablespoons grated Parmesan cheese
½ teaspoon Worcestershire sauce
½ teaspoon salt

TO PREPARE THE STEAKS:
Season each side of each steak abundantly with salt and pepper, and moisten with the olive oil. Let the steaks rest for about 10 minutes.

Preheat the grill, and once it is hot, cook the steaks to medium-rare over medium-high heat, about 3 to 4 minutes per side. Take the steaks off the grill and let them rest, covered, for 3 to 5 minutes.

TO PREPARE THE BALSAMIC-PARMESAN DRESSING:
In a nonstick saucepan over high heat, cook the balsamic vinegar, shallots and garlic for about 2 to 3 minutes, until reduced by half. Let cool.

Pour the balsamic vinegar mixture into a food processor, add the remaining ingredients, and process for about a minute, until the dressing reaches a glossy and smooth consistency.

TO ASSEMBLE THE SALAD:
Dress the baby arugula with 2 to 3 tablespoons of the balsamic-Parmesan dressing. Divide the salad among 4 plates, and then top each salad with shaved Parmesan.

Cut the steaks into ¼-inch slices and divide among the 4 plates, placing the slices either on top of the baby arugula or alongside it. Pour some extra balsamic-Parmesan dressing over the sliced pieces of meat, and serve. Place the extra dressing in a sauce boat and bring it to the table.

CHEF STELLINO'S SUGGESTED WINE PAIRING: *Viña Zaco* Tempranillo Rioja

Easy Chocolate Mousse
Mousse di Cioccolato

NICK STELLINO

Yields 3½ cups

6 ounces white chocolate, cut into small pieces
3 cups heavy cream, divided
3 tablespoons C&H® or Domino® Sugar
1 ounce grated dark chocolate, for topping the mousse

Melt the white chocolate in a double boiler. Whisk in 1 cup of the heavy cream until well blended. Remove from the heat. Let the mixture sit for 20 to 30 minutes to come to room temperature.

Combine 2 cups of the cream and 3 tablespoons sugar in a large, chilled mixing bowl. Use a hand mixer or standing mixer to whip the cream and sugar until stiff peaks form when the beater is stopped and lifted out.

Gently fold a third of the melted white chocolate mixture into the whipped cream. Add the second third; fold in, then add the remainder.

If your mousse becomes soft, it's no cause for alarm. Chill in a bowl for 15 to 20 minutes, and it will be as good as new.

Serve in a big bowl, family style, and top the mousse with the grated dark chocolate.

CHEF'S TIP: For a more elegant presentation, fill a pastry bag equipped with a star tip and pipe the mousse into individual glasses or bowls. Sprinkle with grated white or dark chocolate, and top with sweet whipped cream.

For a variation on this recipe, substitute 6 ounces (1 cup) semisweet chocolate morsels in place of the white chocolate.

CHEF STELLINO'S

SUGGESTED WINE PAIRING: *Codorníu Napa* Grand Reserve Sparkling Wine

Chef Wade Wiestling
The Oceanaire Seafood Room | Minneapolis

Garlic & Lemon Grilled Shrimp with Warm Potato, Arugula & Chorizo Salad

Chinese-Style Tea-Steamed Halibut Steaks with Scallions, Ginger & Fermented Black Beans

Hot Chili Grilled Alaskan Sockeye with Fresh Summer Mango Salsa

Grilled Salmon Salad with Grilled Romaine Hearts, with Blue Cheese & Bacon Vinaigrette

Minnesota-Style Walleye & Wild-Rice Cakes

Warm Banana-White Chocolate Crisp with Macadamia Nut Crumble

NS
Salmon with Vodka & Lemon Sauce
Radicchio & Spinach Sauté with Lemon Zest & Garlic
Fried Capers

Garlic & Lemon Grilled Shrimp with Warm Potato, Arugula & Chorizo Salad

WADE WIESTLING

Serves 4 as an appetizer, 2 as an entrée

This dish makes an easy appetizer or first course, yet it can be easily replicated for an entrée dish. Warm shrimp marinated in lemon and garlic are grilled and served over a warm potato, arugula and chorizo salad. The combination of seafood and sausage makes the dish work. Marinate the shrimp for at least 30 minutes prior, and assemble the potato salad just before grilling the shrimp.

FOR THE GRILLED SHRIMP:
8 large shrimp
2 garlic cloves, peeled and crushed
1 tablespoon fresh lemon zest, finely minced
1 tablespoon Pompeian® Extra Virgin Olive Oil
Dash salt and cracked black pepper to taste

FOR THE WARM POTATO, ARUGULA & CHORIZO SALAD:
6 fingerling potatoes, cooked and cooled
2 Mexican chorizo sausages, cooked and peeled
1 tablespoon Pompeian® Extra Virgin Olive Oil
4 cups arugula, tightly packed
¼ cup smoked paprika vinaigrette (See accompanying recipe.)
Coarse sea salt and black pepper to taste

FOR THE SMOKED PAPRIKA VINAIGRETTE (YIELDS ⅓ CUP):
1 small shallot, peeled and minced
1 clove garlic, peeled and minced
¼ cup Pompeian® Extra Virgin Olive Oil
2 teaspoons lemon juice
2 tablespoons orange juice
2 teaspoons smoked paprika
Salt and pepper to taste

1 teaspoon Meyer lemon-flavored olive oil or Pompeian® Extra Virgin Olive Oil
Pinch smoked paprika
Pinch micro arugula

TO PREPARE THE GRILLED SHRIMP:
Peel and devein the shrimp. In a bowl, toss the shrimp with the garlic, lemon zest, olive oil, and salt and pepper. Let the shrimp marinate at room temperature for 30 minutes or in the refrigerator for longer, up to 8 hours in advance.

Over hot coals or high heat, grill the shrimp, turning them once, for about 4 minutes total—long enough to mark them with nice grill marks. The residual heat will finish the cooking.

TO PREPARE THE WARM POTATO, ARUGULA & CHORIZO SALAD:
Slice the potatoes and chorizo into ½-inch pieces. You should have about equal quantities of potato and sausage.

In a nonstick skillet, heat the oil and sauté the potato and sausage until lightly browned and warmed through. Transfer the potato and sausage slices to a medium-sized bowl. Add the arugula and toss with the vinaigrette to coat. Season, and set aside until ready to assemble.

TO PREPARE THE SMOKED PAPRIKA VINAIGRETTE:
In a small bowl, mix together all the ingredients.

TO SERVE:
Divide the warm potato, arugula and chorizo salad among 4 plates, and top with 2 each (for a first course) of the warm grilled shrimp.

Drizzle with Meyer lemon-flavored olive oil or extra virgin olive oil, sprinkle the plate with smoked paprika, and garnish with the micro greens.

CHEF STELLINO'S SUGGESTED WINE PAIRING: *Durbanville Hills* Sauvignon Blanc

Chinese-Style Tea-Steamed Halibut Steaks
with Scallions, Ginger & Fermented Black Beans

WADE WIESTLING

Serves 4

This is a brightly flavored dish made in the traditional Chinese way; condensed steam mingles with the savory flavorings to make a light sauce that is almost a broth. Almost all Chinese and Japanese recipes for steamed fish suggest cutting deep slashes along the sides of the fish to help the steam penetrate. I've found that the heat penetrates well anyway, so I usually don't bother.

2 tablespoons preserved black beans (Available at many upscale grocers and Asian specialty markets.)
4 tablespoons dark soy sauce
¼ cup Chinese rice wine or Spanish dry sherry
1 tablespoon Japanese dark sesame oil
½ tablespoon C&H® or Domino® Sugar
1 3-inch piece fresh ginger, peeled
4 8-ounce fresh Alaskan halibut steaks
4 scallions, including green parts, cut into 1-inch lengths
2 tea bags (Chinese black tea, bags cut open and tea leaves reserved)

Rinse the black beans in a strainer for about 1 minute under cold running water and chop coarsely. Combine the beans with the soy sauce, rice wine, sesame oil and sugar in a small bowl.

Slice the ginger into ⅛-inch-thick rounds and then into a fine julienne.

Place the halibut steaks on a plate or in a pie tin with a deep enough rim to hold the soy sauce mixture and any juices released by the fish. Pour on the soy sauce mixture and sprinkle the fish with the ginger, scallions and tea leaves.

Bring a quart of water to a rolling boil in the base of a steamer, set the plate in the top, and cover tightly. Steam for 8 minutes per inch of thickness. Check for doneness with a paring knife along the thickest part of the fillet. The fish should flake easily. Turn off the heat, remove the lid, and let the steam dissipate for a minute before reaching in and pulling out the plate. Be careful not to tilt the plate and spill the sauce. Make sure the fish is cooked to your liking.

Spoon the sauce, ginger and scallions over the fish and serve immediately with steamed white rice.

CHEF STELLINO'S SUGGESTED WINE PAIRING: *Viña Pomal* Rioja Crianza

Hot Chili Grilled Alaskan Sockeye with Fresh Summer Mango Salsa

WADE WIESTLING

Serves 4

Sockeye salmon, also known as red salmon for their brilliant red flesh color, average about 5 to 8 pounds. The sockeye's deep red meat has only moderate oil content and is firmer-textured and breaks into smaller flakes, making it a natural star for summer grilling, smoking and salad recipes. Sockeye run from late spring through late summer, with June, July and early August being the best time of year to enjoy these beautiful wild salmon...fresh!

This is an easy, quick recipe that takes advantage of the sockeye's lower oil content and highlights the salmon's robust flavor without overpowering it. Happy grilling!

4 8-ounce fresh wild Alaskan sockeye fillets, skin on

FOR THE SALMON RUB:
2 tablespoons **Asian hot chili oil** (Available at many upscale grocers and Asian specialty markets.)
2 tablespoons fresh-squeezed lime juice
2 tablespoons mint, finely chopped
1 tablespoon fresh ginger, grated
1 teaspoon fresh garlic, minced
Pinch crushed red pepper flakes
Salt and fresh-ground pepper to taste

FOR THE SUMMER MANGO SALSA:
1 tomato, seeded and diced
1 mango, peeled and diced
¼ cup green onion, chopped
1 tablespoon mint, chopped
1 tablespoon Thai basil, chopped
1 tablespoon **reserved salmon rub mixture** (See recipe.)
Salt and fresh-ground pepper to taste

TO PREPARE THE SALMON RUB:
Mix together all of the salmon rub ingredients in a small bowl. Reserve 1 tablespoon of this mixture to season the salsa.

TO PREPARE THE SOCKEYE FILLETS:
Preheat the barbecue grill to medium-high; oil the grill.

Smear the salmon rub mixture over the flesh side of the salmon, and rub it into the salmon flesh. Let stand for 5 minutes.

Sear the salmon, flesh side down, for 2 minutes. Turn the salmon over, cover the grill, and cook another 6 to 8 minutes, until the salmon just flakes when pressed with a fork.

Alternatively, place the salmon on the grill, skin side down, and cook, covered, for 8 to 12 minutes, until the skin is charred and crisp and easily removed.

TO PREPARE THE SUMMER MANGO SALSA:
Combine and toss all the salsa ingredients just before serving. Season the salsa with the reserved salmon rub.

TO SERVE:
Serve the sockeye fillets warm, topped with summer mango salsa and the juices.

CHEF STELLINO'S SUGGESTED WINE PAIRING: *Artesa* Carneros Chardonnay

Chef Wiestling UNSCRIPTED

WHY DO YOU DO WHAT YOU DO?

First and foremost, for my family—my beautiful wife and our son Cooper. They keep me motivated to go out and do my best every day. Secondly, I love the hospitality business and taking care of people; whether my employees or our valued guests, I relish looking after them to be sure their needs are met and they are happy when they leave. Hospitality runs through my veins. I'm a mother hen.

WHAT IS YOUR FIRST FOOD MEMORY?

So many fond food memories growing up. Sunday dinners were always fun; my grandparents had no issues with pulling every pot, every pan, every plate out of the cupboards to pull together a huge feast for eight to 10 people every Sunday. The kitchen was small, and a small disaster afterwards, and everybody pitched in. Growing up on the East Coast, I vividly remember going out and buying bushels of top neck clams at the local seafood market, bringing them home, dumping them in the utility sink, and scrubbing them, steaming them open and preparing stuffed clams for the feast. The men in the family would have a contest to see who could stack up the most empty clam shells as they powered down stuffed clams.

WHAT IS YOUR FAVORITE DISH TO EAT? TO PREPARE?

Italian food and cooking is what I fall back on. I love to prepare and eat simple pasta dishes that satisfy and nourish. In Italian cooking, it's all about the pasta...

IS THERE A FOOD YOU HATE/DON'T LIKE?

I really do eat and enjoy most everything you put in front of me, but monkfish liver and stinging nettles... I will never understand how they came to be such "foodie" ingredients.

IF YOU COULD HAVE ONLY ONE FOOD FOR THE REST OF YOUR LIFE, WHAT WOULD THAT FOOD BE?

See question #3. I could enjoy pasta, salad and wine for the rest of my life. And fresh seafood, of course...

WHAT OR WHO INSPIRES YOU?

Inspiration comes from everywhere, whether it's the changing of the seasons, working alongside other talented chefs, eating out at other establishments, or traveling throughout the country. One major source of inspiration for me (other than my family) is to be inspiring to others that I have an opportunity to work with. I want to inspire them to be better cooks, better leaders and better human beings.

Grilled Salmon Salad with Grilled Romaine Hearts, with Blue Cheese & Bacon Vinaigrette

WADE WIESTLING

Serves 4

In a word, nothing says summer like grilling. Summer means lighting up that grill and preparing all your fresh summer salmon. Since you have all that fire, why not grill your salad, too? This recipe takes advantage of the grill for both the salmon AND the romaine lettuce, which make a nice, smoky counterpart to sharp, pungent blue cheese in the dressing. The grilled flavor is easily imparted to the romaine lettuce, and the blue cheese and bacon imbue the dish with a terrific woodsy flavor. Great with all kinds of grilled meats and seafood.

FOR THE SALMON:
4 fresh salmon fillets, 8 ounces each
1 teaspoon Pompeian® Extra Virgin Olive Oil
2 teaspoons coarse sea salt
2 teaspoons fresh-ground black pepper

FOR THE VINAIGRETTE:
3 tablespoons Pompeian® Extra Virgin Olive Oil, divided
¾ cup red onion, diced
½ pound smoked bacon, diced
2 tablespoons Pompeian® Red Wine Vinegar
1 teaspoon fresh thyme, minced
1 tablespoon honey

FOR THE GRILLED ROMAINE HEARTS:
2 romaine hearts, cut in half lengthwise, cores kept intact
2 tablespoons Pompeian® Extra Virgin Olive Oil
Salt and cracked black pepper to taste

½ cup blue cheese, crumbled
Green-onion curls, for garnish
Flatbread

Preheat the grill to medium-high heat (400 degrees).

TO PREPARE THE VINAIGRETTE:
Heat 1 tablespoon extra virgin olive oil in a sauté pan over medium-high heat. Add the onions and bacon, and cook until the bacon is crispy. To the same pan add the red wine vinegar, thyme and honey, and bring up to a simmer. Remove from the heat; drizzle in 2 tablespoons extra virgin olive oil and stir to combine. Set aside and keep warm.

TO PREPARE THE SALMON:
Brush the salmon with olive oil and season with salt and black pepper. Grill for 2 to 3 minutes. Turn the salmon 45 degrees and continue to grill for 2 to 3 minutes longer. Flip the salmon over and grill for 3 to 4 minutes longer. If you like your salmon slightly underdone, remove 2 to 3 minutes after flipping it over.

TO PREPARE THE GRILLED ROMAINE HEARTS:
Rinse and pat dry the lettuce. Brush the surface with olive oil, and season with salt and pepper. Grill the lettuce for about 2 to 3 minutes per side (4 to 6 minutes total), turning occasionally to keep it from getting too charred and crispy.

TO SERVE:
Arrange the lettuce hearts on dinner plates, and arrange the salmon on the grilled lettuce hearts. Stir the warm bacon vinaigrette and drizzle it over the salmon and lettuce. Sprinkle with blue cheese crumbles. Garnish the dish with green-onion curls, and serve with warm flatbread.

CHEF STELLINO'S SUGGESTED WINE PAIRING: *Bodega Septima* Chardonnay

Minnesota-Style Walleye & Wild-Rice Cakes

WADE WIESTLING

Serves 4 as an entrée (makes 8 4-ounce cakes)

Hands down, the most-requested recipe at The Oceanaire Seafood Room is our Crab Cake recipe. That is a trade secret that we cannot part with. So I give you this: a Minnesota variation of that recipe utilizing fresh walleye and wild rice, both native products of Minnesota. You can bake these cakes on an aluminum foil-lined baking sheet on your gas grill—great for when you are at the lake or in your backyard. Enjoy!

1 pound skinless walleye fillets, cooked and chilled (See accompanying recipe.)
Salt and pepper
1 lemon
Artesa Carneros Chardonnay

FOR THE WILD-RICE CAKES:
1 cup wild rice, cooked (well done) **and cooled** (See accompanying recipe.)
Salt to taste
Beef or chicken broth (optional)
2 eggs, whole
1 cup mayonnaise
½ teaspoon dry mustard
2 teaspoons Old Bay Seasoning, plus more to taste
1 tablespoon parsley, freshly chopped
¼ cup yellow onion, finely chopped
5 slices white sandwich bread
1 ounce whole butter, melted

Homemade tartar sauce
Mixed field greens with vinaigrette

TO PREPARE THE COOKED WALLEYE FILLETS:
Line a baking sheet with the walleye fillets and season them with salt and pepper; squeeze the juice of 1 lemon over the fillets and sprinkle them with Chardonnay. Bake at 350 degrees for 10 to 13 minutes, until just cooked through. Chill the fillets and flake them into a mixing bowl, carefully removing any bones.

TO PREPARE THE COOKED WILD RICE (YIELDS 2 CUPS):

Wash ½ cup uncooked wild rice and rinse it thoroughly under cool running water. Add the rice to 4 cups boiling water, salted to taste, in a heavy saucepan. (For additional flavor, try cooking the rice in beef or chicken broth.) Return the water to a boil, and stir. Reduce the heat and simmer, covered, 50 to 60 minutes, or just until the kernels puff open like popcorn. Uncover the pan and fluff the rice with a table fork. Simmer 5 additional minutes. Drain any excess liquid, and allow the rice to cool.

TO PREPARE THE WILD-RICE CAKES:

In a large mixing bowl, make a dressing by mixing together the eggs, mayo, mustard, 2 teaspoons Old Bay, parsley and onion. Keep the dressing chilled.

Cut the crust from the bread slices and cut into small (½-inch) cubes.

In another large mixing bowl, add the bread cubes and a little over half of the dressing, reserving the remaining dressing for additional use as needed. Blend the two ingredients together until the dressing has been absorbed by the bread. You may need to add more dressing at this point.

Gently mix the cooked walleye and the cooked wild rice with the above mixture, being careful to keep the flaked pieces of fish intact. The mixture should hold its shape when formed into a ball with your hand. If it is too loose, you may need to add more bread; if it is too tight, you may need to add more dressing.

Form the balls into small cakes of the desired size (4- to 5-ounce cakes for service as entrées or appetizers, or 1-ounce cakes for a passed hors d'oeuvre). Place the cakes on a greased cookie sheet or sheet pan, top with a small amount of melted butter seasoned with Old Bay, and place in a 400-degree oven for 10 to 12 minutes, until golden brown.

Serve with homemade tartar sauce and a light field-greens salad.

CHEF STELLINO'S SUGGESTED WINE PAIRING: *Voga* Pinot Grigio

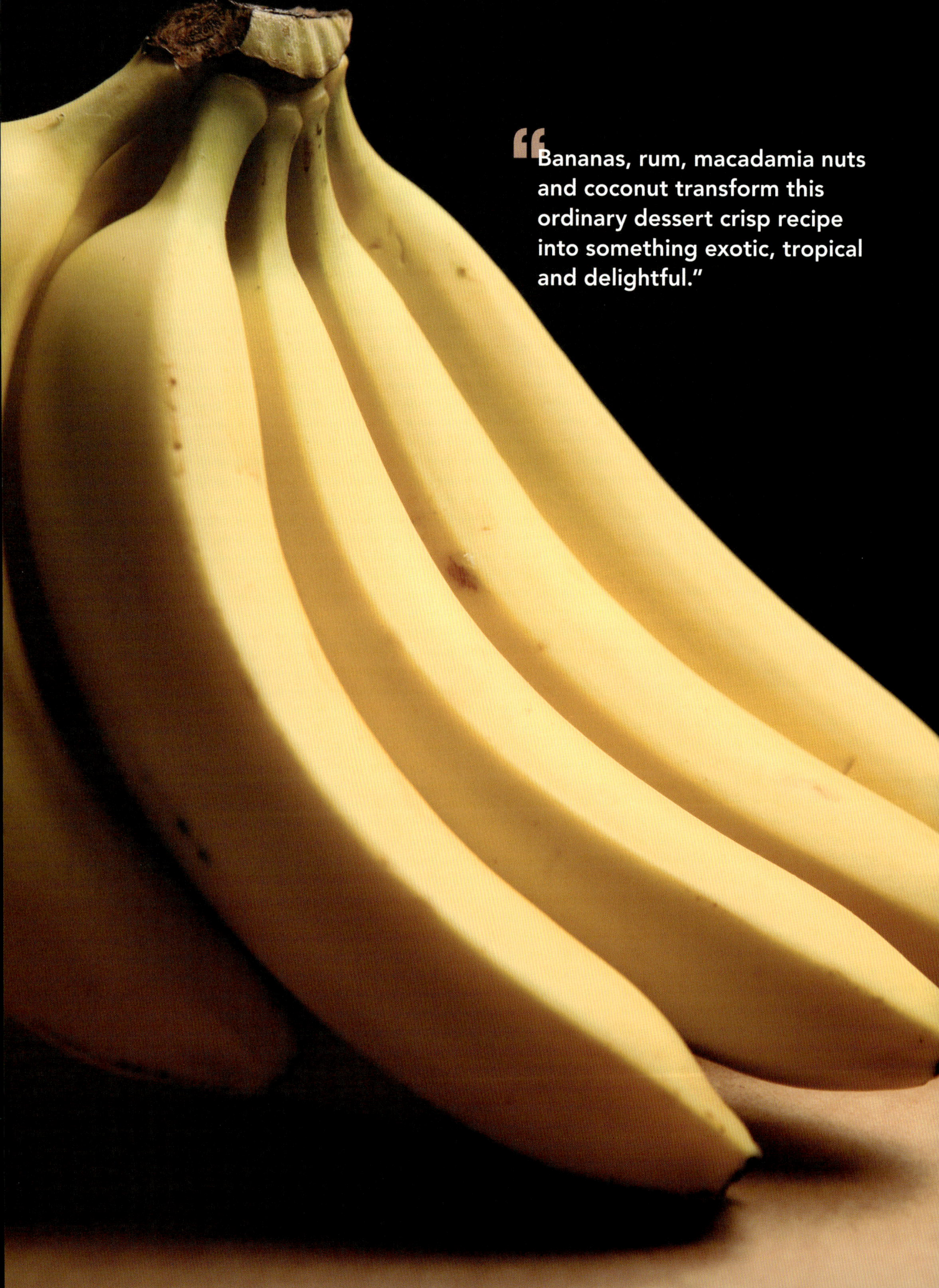

"Bananas, rum, macadamia nuts and coconut transform this ordinary dessert crisp recipe into something exotic, tropical and delightful."

Warm Banana-White Chocolate Crisp with Macadamia Nut Crumble

WADE WIESTLING

Serves 4 to 6

Delicious when paired with vanilla ice cream, this dessert is like a vacation in and of itself. You can bake it in an 8-inch square dish, or in individual-size baking dishes for a more formal presentation.

6 cups ripe, firm bananas, sliced
1 cup C&H® or Domino® Sugar
1 tablespoon dark rum
1 tablespoon banana liqueur
¼ teaspoon ground nutmeg
½ teaspoon ground cinnamon
1 cup white chocolate chips, divided
½ cup C&H® Golden Brown Sugar or Domino® Light Brown Sugar, firmly packed
1 cup all-purpose flour
1 cup rolled oats
½ cup macadamia nuts, coarsely chopped
3 tablespoons coconut, shredded
½ teaspoon salt
¾ cup whole unsalted butter, cold, cut into ½-inch dice

Preheat the oven to 375 degrees. Grease an 8-inch square dish, or 4 to 6 individual dessert ramekins.

Combine the bananas, sugar, rum, banana liqueur, nutmeg and cinnamon, and stir to combine. Add ¾ cup white chocolate chips, and toss to combine.

Mix the brown sugar, flour, oats, macadamia nuts, coconut, ¼ cup white chocolate chips and the salt; stir well to combine. Cut in the cold diced butter until it forms crumbs. Loosely scatter the mixture over the banana mixture and bake for 20 to 30 minutes, or until browned.

Allow the crisp to cool for 15 minutes, and serve warm with vanilla ice cream or plain whipped cream.

CHEF STELLINO'S SUGGESTED WINE PAIRING: *Umberto Fiore* Moscato d'Asti

Salmon with Vodka & Lemon Sauce

NICK STELLINO

Serves 4

¼ teaspoon salt
¼ teaspoon pepper
1 teaspoon onion powder
¼ teaspoon paprika
4 fillets of salmon, 4 to 5 ounces each
2 tablespoons Pompeian® Extra Light Tasting Olive Oil
1 tablespoon softened butter
1 recipe vodka and lemon sauce (See accompanying recipe.)
1 recipe Radicchio & Spinach Sauté with Lemon Zest & Garlic (See recipe on page 207.)
2 tablespoons Fried Capers (See recipe on page 207.)

FOR THE VODKA & LEMON SAUCE:
2 tablespoons Pompeian® Extra Light Tasting Olive Oil
1 carrot, peeled and diced
1 celery stalk, diced
1 small white onion, peeled and chopped
1 garlic clove, finely chopped
1 tablespoon fresh dill, chopped
2 teaspoons capers
1 cup Tomato Sauce (See recipe on page 89.)
1 tablespoon C&H® or Domino® Organic Agave Nectar, or 1 tablespoon C&H® or Domino® Sugar
4 tablespoons vodka
1 cup clam juice
3 cups chicken stock
¼ cup lemon juice
4 tablespoons whipping cream
2 tablespoons water
1 teaspoon cornstarch
3 tablespoons softened butter
2 tablespoons parsley, chopped, for garnish

TO PREPARE THE SALMON:
Make a spice mixture with the salt, pepper, onion powder and paprika. Sprinkle gently over both sides of the salmon fillets.

In a nonstick sauté pan, bring the olive oil to a sizzle over medium-high heat. Reduce the heat to low and add the salmon fillets. Cook exactly 2 minutes per side. During the last 2 minutes of cooking, add the softened butter to the fish to baste and glaze it.

TO PREPARE THE VODKA & LEMON SAUCE:

In a saucepan, add the olive oil and cook over medium-high heat until it starts to sizzle.

Add the carrot, celery, white onion, garlic, dill, capers, tomato sauce and agave nectar. Reduce the heat to medium and cook, stirring well, for 3 to 4 minutes.

Add the vodka and reduce by half (about 2 to 3 minutes), then add the clam juice, chicken stock and lemon juice. Bring to a boil over high heat, then reduce the heat to medium-low and add the whipping cream. Stir well and cook the sauce, covered, over low heat for 45 to 50 minutes.

Strain the sauce, bring to a boil over medium-high heat, and add a slurry made of 2 tablespoons of water and 1 teaspoon of cornstarch. Stir well and reduce by a third (about 5 to 6 minutes), then reduce the heat to low and cook the sauce, uncovered, for 10 more minutes.

Bring the sauce to a boil and add 3 tablespoons of softened butter. Turn off the heat and incorporate the butter in the sauce, stirring well.

TO SERVE:

Serve the salmon in a dish, topped with the vodka and lemon sauce, and garnished with parsley. Enjoy with Radicchio & Spinach Sauté and Fried Capers. (See recipes on page 207.)

CHEF STELLINO'S SUGGESTED WINE PAIRING: *Artesa* Estate Reserve Pinot Noir

Radicchio & Spinach Sauté with Lemon Zest & Garlic

NICK STELLINO

Serves 4

3 tablespoons Pompeian® Extra Virgin Olive Oil
1 teaspoon lemon zest
2 teaspoons shallots, chopped
2 teaspoons garlic, chopped
1 cup radicchio, cored and thinly sliced
½ teaspoon salt
½ teaspoon pepper
4 ounces baby spinach leaves

In a 12-inch sauté pan, cook the oil over medium-high heat for 1 to 2 minutes until it starts to sizzle.

Add the lemon zest, shallots and garlic, and cook over medium heat for 1 minute.

Add the radicchio and cook, stirring well, for 1 more minute. Add the salt and the pepper, and stir well.

Turn off the heat, add the spinach, and mix all the ingredients together, stirring well. Serve at once.

CHEF'S TIP: Alternatively, once you have finished cooking the radicchio, place the spinach in a large stainless-steel bowl and pour the lemon zest-and-garlic mixture over it. Mix well, and serve at once.

Fried Capers

NICK STELLINO

Serves 4

2 tablespoons Pompeian® Extra Light Tasting Olive Oil
2 tablespoons capers, drained, washed and dried

Cook the olive oil over medium-high heat for 1 to 2 minutes until it starts to sizzle. Reduce the heat to medium-low, add the capers, and fry, stirring well, for 1 to 2 minutes.

Let the capers cool on a dish lined with a paper towel. Serve while still warm.

Chef Jason Wilson
Crush | Seattle

- Stove-Top Braised Octopus
- Cauliflower Tabouleh
- Nine-Spice Scallops
- Cucumber-Melon Salad with Minted Ricotta
- Pork Ragù
- Slow-Braised Short Ribs with Parsley Pistou

NS
- Pork Chops with Zenzero Sauce
- Roasted Asparagus with Parmesan Cheese

Stove-Top Braised Octopus

JASON WILSON

Serves 6

4 pounds fresh octopus (or frozen, defrosted)
¼ cup Pompeian® Extra Virgin Olive Oil
1 stalk celery, sliced ¼ inch thick, in half-rings
5 cloves garlic, peeled and smashed (not chopped)
¼ cup onions, rough-chopped
½ bunch Italian parsley, rough-chopped
1 tablespoon chili flakes
2 bay leaves
1 teaspoon pimenton (smoked paprika)
1 teaspoon fennel seeds
2 tablespoons kosher salt

Wrap the octopus in cheesecloth or a kitchen towel and pound it with a carpaccio mallet or a hammer for 5 minutes to start the tenderizing process. Unwrap the octopus from the cheesecloth and place it in a large bowl. Allow cold water to slowly run over the bowl and octopus for 10 minutes, rinsing the octopus. Then remove the octopus from the water and refrigerate.

In a large sauce- or stockpot, simmer the olive oil, celery, garlic and onions until fragrant, roughly 8 minutes on medium-high heat. Add the octopus and simmer for 10 minutes. Add the remaining ingredients (except kosher salt) and cover; simmer for 1½ hours on low heat. Allow the octopus to cool in the liquid for 30 minutes. Add the kosher salt while it's cooling.

Slice thinly to serve in a salad or with marinated antipasti, or sauté to serve the tentacles with Cauliflower Tabouleh. (See recipe on page 210.)

**CHEF STELLINO'S
SUGGESTED WINE PAIRING:** *Ca'Montini* Pinot Grigio

Cauliflower Tabouleh

JASON WILSON

Serves 6

1 ounce garlic, chopped
2 ounces shallots, finely chopped
3 ounces Pompeian® Extra Virgin Olive Oil
4 ounces finely chopped tomato—heirloom if possible—no seeds
2 ounces kosher salt, plus 1 pinch
2½ pounds organic cauliflower, whole heads
2 ounces preserved lemon, finely chopped
½ bunch parsley, chopped well
½ bunch chives, chopped
⅛ bunch mint, chopped
½ ounce toasted and ground cumin seeds
¼ ounce smoked paprika
2 ounces sherry vinegar (Or substitute Pompeian® Pomegranate Infused White Balsamic Vinegar.)
1 ounce orange juice

In a small saucepan on medium heat, simmer the garlic and shallots in the olive oil until they are fragrant and golden brown, 2 to 3 minutes. Pour the mixture into a mixing bowl, then add the tomato and a pinch of salt.

On a box grater, grate the cauliflower into fine pieces over a stainless-steel bowl. Place on a cutting board and chop very finely so that the cauliflower resembles a couscous grain size. Add the 2 ounces kosher salt to the cauliflower and allow to marinate 30 minutes. After marinating in the salt, drain off any water and place the cauliflower in the stainless-steel bowl. Mix all the remaining ingredients well and add to the cauliflower along with the garlic-shallot-tomato mixture. Adjust the seasoning if needed.

CHEF STELLINO'S SUGGESTED WINE PAIRING: *Belmondo* Pinot Grigio

Nine-Spice Scallops

JASON WILSON

Serves 6

12 large sea scallops (U-10 count)
1 teaspoon ground coriander
½ teaspoon ground fennel
½ teaspoon ground cinnamon
½ teaspoon ground black pepper
½ teaspoon ground cloves
½ teaspoon ground cumin
½ teaspoon ground chili flakes
½ teaspoon paprika (smoked, if possible)
6 leaves fresh basil, chopped fine
6 leaves fresh mint, chopped fine
2 tablespoons kosher salt
3 tablespoons Pompeian® Extra Light Tasting Olive Oil, for sautéing

In a small sauté pan, toast all the dry spices (through paprika) on medium heat for 1 to 2 minutes until aromatic. Add the chopped fresh herbs and mix well.

Remove the "feet" from the scallops and ensure the scallops are clean. Season the scallops with the kosher salt and the spice mixture.

On medium-high heat in a large sauté pan, sear the scallops in the olive oil until they are golden brown, roughly 5 to 6 minutes. Once browned, turn them over and sear another 45 seconds.

Serve the scallops over Cucumber-Melon Salad (see recipe on page 213) for a complete entrée.

CHEF STELLINO'S SUGGESTED WINE PAIRING: *Léon Beyer* Riesling

Cucumber-Melon Salad (FACING PAGE)
Durbanville Hills Sauvignon Blanc

Cucumber-Melon Salad with Minted Ricotta

JASON WILSON

Serves 6

6 slices prosciutto
3 tablespoons corn syrup
2 tablespoons lime juice
⅓ cup rice wine vinegar
1 red jalapeño pepper, seeds removed, chopped fine
12 leaves fresh basil
½ honeydew melon
½ cantaloupe
½ English cucumber, peeled, seeded and sliced into half-moons
1 head Belgian endive
1 bunch mint
¼ cup Pompeian® Extra Virgin Olive Oil
1 teaspoon cracked pepper
2 tablespoons kosher salt
½ pound fresh ricotta
Sea salt as needed, for garnish

Preheat the oven to 350 degrees.

Place the strips of prosciutto on a parchment-lined half sheet (baking) pan; place another sheet of parchment on top and another baking pan on top of it. Place the "sandwich" of pans in the oven for 25 minutes. Rotate as needed. Remove from the oven, lift the top pan and parchment carefully, turn the prosciutto over with a spatula, and place the parchment and pan on top again. Bake another 7 minutes. Remove from the oven and place the prosciutto "chips" on a cooling rack to dry.

In a small saucepan, simmer the corn syrup, lime juice, rice wine vinegar and jalapeño. Reduce the volume by half. Allow the mixture time to cool.

Chop the basil roughly. Cut the melon into 1-inch cubes. Combine the melon, basil and cucumber, and pour the lime juice-and-vinegar mixture over them. Allow to marinate for 20 minutes.

Slice the endive into rough 1- to 1½-inch chunks.

Chop the mint very, very finely. Add the mint, olive oil, pepper and kosher salt to a mixing bowl with the ricotta and mix thoroughly. (KitchenAid mixers are great for this!)

To serve, toss the melon, basil and cucumber together with the endive, spoon the ricotta mixture onto a plate, and "smear" it to evenly distribute the cheese. Place the salad on top of the ricotta mixture, and garnish with the prosciutto chips and sea salt. For a complete entrée, serve the salad with Nine-Spice Scallops. (See recipe on page 212.)

Pork Ragù

JASON WILSON

Serves 6 (Ingredients can be reduced by 25 percent to serve 4.)

4 pounds fresh natural pork butt, boneless, large-chopped
1 cup Pompeian® Extra Virgin Olive Oil
Salt and pepper as needed
2 yellow onions, cut into small dice
1 leek, cut into small dice
1 fennel bulb, cut into small dice
2 stalks celery, cut into small dice
5 cloves garlic, sliced
1 cup Elements by Artesa Cabernet Sauvignon
1 4-ounce jar piquillo peppers
1 quart canned crushed tomatoes
¼ cup pitted olives (Cerignola or similar green)
2 quarts chicken stock
2 tablespoons ground cumin
1 tablespoon ground fennel
1 tablespoon ground coriander
2 tablespoons chopped marjoram and rosemary
2 bay leaves

In a large sauce pot or brazier pan (6 quarts or so) on medium-high heat, sear the pork in the olive oil until dark brown. Season the meat with salt and pepper to taste.

When the meat is well browned, add the diced vegetables and garlic, and continue to brown. When the vegetables have sweated well and are evenly brown, deglaze with red wine and reduce by half. Add the peppers, tomatoes and olives, and cook for 15 minutes. Add the stock and simmer for 40 minutes. Finish with salt and pepper to taste and the herbs.

Use the ragù to dress the DaVinci® pasta of your choice.

CHEF STELLINO'S SUGGESTED WINE PAIRING: *Elements by Artesa* Red Wine

Chef Wilson UNSCRIPTED

WHY DO YOU DO WHAT YOU DO?
I am a chef because I enjoy giving, creating and being a part of memories. I enjoy the seasons and sharing my inspirations with others.

WHAT IS YOUR FIRST FOOD MEMORY?
First food memories would be bacon-and-vinegar green beans at my grandma's or brown-trout sandwiches.

WHAT IS YOUR FAVORITE DISH TO EAT? TO PREPARE?
To eat, I love chocolate, raw fish and sea urchin. To prepare, I love roasting a chicken and making a sandwich.

IS THERE A FOOD YOU HATE/DON'T LIKE?
There is none.

IF YOU COULD HAVE ONLY ONE FOOD FOR THE REST OF YOUR LIFE, WHAT WOULD THAT FOOD BE?
One food for the rest of my life? Tomatoes.

WHAT OR WHO INSPIRES YOU?
The seasons inspire, and people invigorate.

Slow-Braised Short Ribs with Parsley Pistou

JASON WILSON

Serves 4 to 6

4 pounds bone-in beef short ribs, 3-inch cut
Kosher salt and pepper to taste
½ bunch thyme
½ bunch rosemary
5 bay leaves
1 750-ml bottle Artesa Carneros Pinot Noir
Pompeian® Extra Virgin Olive Oil
3 cups large-chopped mirepoix (3 parts onion, 2 parts carrot, 1 part celery)
2 dried porcini mushrooms
2 quarts veal stock (Or substitute chicken stock.)

FOR THE PARSLEY PISTOU:
1 bunch fresh Italian parsley
Ice water
1 cup (approximately) freshly grated horseradish root
Salt to taste
⅓ cup truffle oil (Or substitute Pompeian® Extra Virgin Olive Oil.)

Season the short ribs liberally with salt and pepper.

Place the ribs in a large container. Cover with the herbs and pour the red wine over all. Marinate for at least 12 hours.

Remove the ribs, reserving the marinade. In a large cast-iron or heavy-bottomed skillet, add enough extra virgin olive oil to equal ¼ inch. Sear the ribs on high heat until dark brown on all sides. Remove the ribs when good and dark, and place in a brazier or hotel pan. Top with the herbs used in marinating.

Pour the reserved red wine marinade into a sauce pot. Bring the wine to a simmer slowly and skim off any impurities; reduce to half the original volume.

In the same skillet that you used to sear the ribs, sauté the mirepoix veggies and the porcini until brown. Pour the reduced wine over the veggies and bring up to a simmer. Remove the ribs from the brazier pan and add them to the skillet; top with the thyme sprigs, rosemary and bay leaves, and enough veal stock just to cover. Bring up to a simmer, then transfer everything to the brazier pan and place in a 375-degree oven for 4 hours, covered with parchment and foil.

When the ribs are tender, allow 30 minutes for them to cool, and then remove from the braising liquid. Strain the liquid into a stainless-steel sauce pot and reduce very slowly, skimming the fat and impurities, until one-quarter of the original liquid is left. Place the ribs back in the sauce and simmer, covered, until they are nicely glazed with the sauce.

TO PREPARE THE PARSLEY PISTOU:
Leave the rubber band on the bottom of the parsley. Wash upside-down and, holding the parsley by the stem with tongs, blanch in boiling salted water for about 10 seconds. Allow to rest in ice water, and press out the water after it's cooled down. Chop the leaves and pat dry with a towel.

Put the leaves into a blender and add an equal part grated horseradish. Salt to taste, and add truffle oil. Blend until smooth and combined to make an even puree. Add a small amount of water if necessary to thin to sauce consistency.

TO SERVE:
Serve the ribs with parsley pistou, baby carrots that have been blanched and sautéed in butter, and potato puree. (Use Yukon Gold potatoes, boiled in their skins, peeled, and passed through a food mill, then a fine strainer; blend with cream and butter.)

CHEF STELLINO'S SUGGESTED WINE PAIRING: *Legaris* Ribera del Duero Crianza

Pork Chops with Zenzero Sauce

NICK STELLINO

Serves 4

4 pork chops, bone-in, center-cut, totaling 2 to 2½ pounds
Salt and pepper to taste
3 tablespoons Pompeian® Extra Light Tasting Olive Oil
3 tablespoons softened butter (optional)

FOR THE MARINADE:
2 cups water
2 tablespoons C&H® or Domino® Sugar
1 tablespoon salt

FOR THE ZENZERO SAUCE:
4 tablespoons Pompeian® Extra Virgin Olive Oil
¼ teaspoon red pepper flakes (optional)
1 medium white onion, finely chopped
1 medium carrot, finely chopped
1 stalk celery, finely chopped
2 tablespoons fresh ginger, chopped
2 tablespoons fresh basil, chopped
2 tablespoons fresh rosemary leaves, loosely packed
2 garlic cloves, finely chopped
2 tablespoons ketchup
½ cup sherry
1 tablespoon Worcestershire sauce
2 cups apple juice
2 cups chicken stock
Salt and pepper to taste

Place the pork chops in a resealable plastic bag. Place the water, sugar and salt for the marinade in a small bowl, stir well to incorporate, and pour over the pork chops in the bag. Seal the bag shut and marinate the pork chops for at least 5 hours, or preferably overnight.

Make the zenzero sauce (see accompanying recipe) and keep warm.

Preheat the barbecue. If using a gas model, set all the burners to high and close the cover until the internal temperature reaches 500 degrees.

Take the chops out of the marinade and pat dry with a paper towel. Discard the marinade. Sprinkle the chops with salt and pepper to taste. Brush each side of the pork chops with the extra light tasting olive oil. You do not need to use all of it.

Reduce the heat on the grill to medium and cook the chops for 3 to 4 minutes per side with the cover down. (Alternatively, you can cook the chops in a hot sauté pan with 1 tablespoon extra light tasting olive oil over medium-high heat for 3 to 4 minutes per side.) Place the chops on a tray and cover with foil.

Bring the zenzero sauce to a boil in a saucepan large enough to hold all of the chops. Add the chops and reduce the heat to a simmer. Cook the chops, basting them with the sauce, for 2 to 3 more minutes over medium-low heat.

Place each chop in an individual serving dish. Bring the sauce to a boil over high heat, and cook for 1 to 2 more minutes until it thickens to the desired consistency. Add the optional butter, swirling it in the pan until it melts completely. Pour the zenzero sauce over the chops, and serve. Roasted Asparagus with Parmesan Cheese (see recipe on page 223) makes a perfect accompaniment.

TO PREPARE THE ZENZERO SAUCE:
Pour the extra virgin olive oil into a large saucepan and cook over high heat until it starts to sizzle. Add the optional red pepper flakes, the white onion, carrot, celery, ginger and fresh herbs; reduce the heat to medium and cook, stirring well, for 3 to 4 minutes until the onion starts to soften. Add the garlic and the ketchup, and cook for 1 more minute, stirring well.

Add the sherry and Worcestershire sauce, and increase the heat to high. Stir well until reduced by two-thirds, about 3 to 4 minutes. Add the apple juice and chicken stock; bring to a boil, and cover. Reduce the heat to low and cook for 40 minutes.

Strain the sauce through a fine sieve, pushing the pulp through with a rubber spatula and trying to extract as much liquid as possible.

Bring the strained sauce to a boil over high heat. Reduce the heat to medium and cook for 8 to 10 minutes until the liquid reduces by about one-third and reaches a thick consistency. Add salt and pepper to taste. Keep warm until ready to use, or store, covered, in the refrigerator once it cools down. The sauce can be made up to 2 days ahead.

CHEF STELLINO'S SUGGESTED WINE PAIRING: *Artesa* Artisan Series Napa Valley Merlot

Roasted Asparagus with Parmesan Cheese

NICK STELLINO

Serves 4

1 pound fresh asparagus spears
2 tablespoons Pompeian® Extra Light Tasting Olive Oil
½ teaspoon salt
½ teaspoon ground pepper
2 tablespoons shallots, chopped
2 tablespoons red bell pepper, finely diced
1 tablespoon rosemary, chopped
½ teaspoon onion powder
¼ teaspoon paprika
3 tablespoons chicken stock or water
3 tablespoons grated Parmesan cheese

Preheat the oven to 450 degrees.

In a large bowl, mix together all the ingredients except the stock and the Parmesan.

Place the asparagus mixture in a baking dish. Add the stock, and bake in the oven for 12 minutes at 400 degrees. (Reduce the oven temperature to 400 just before placing the dish in the oven.)

Sprinkle the grated Parmesan over the roasted asparagus and bake for 5 more minutes.

Take out of the oven and serve with your favorite meal.

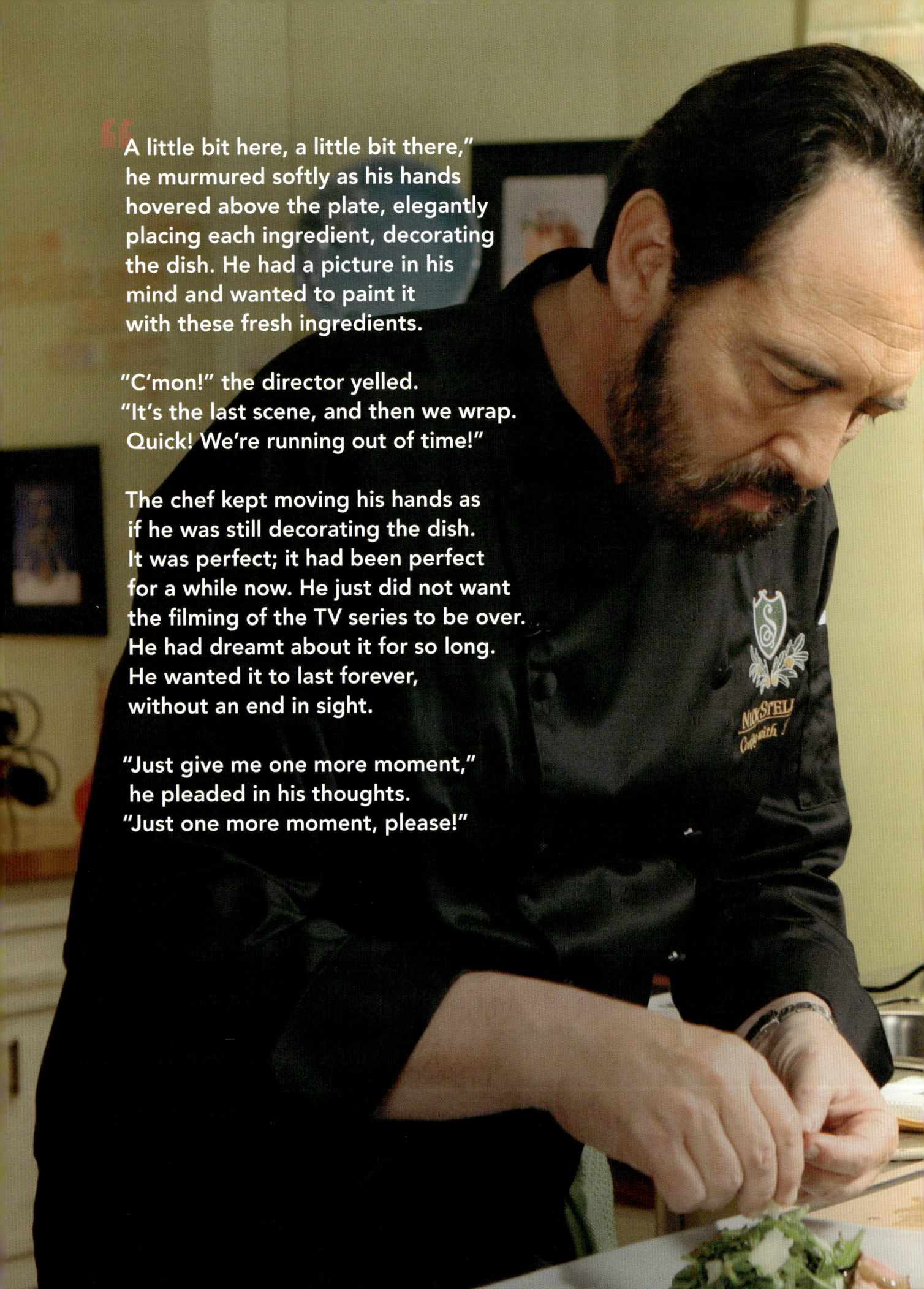

"A little bit here, a little bit there," he murmured softly as his hands hovered above the plate, elegantly placing each ingredient, decorating the dish. He had a picture in his mind and wanted to paint it with these fresh ingredients.

"C'mon!" the director yelled. "It's the last scene, and then we wrap. Quick! We're running out of time!"

The chef kept moving his hands as if he was still decorating the dish. It was perfect; it had been perfect for a while now. He just did not want the filming of the TV series to be over. He had dreamt about it for so long. He wanted it to last forever, without an end in sight.

"Just give me one more moment," he pleaded in his thoughts. "Just one more moment, please!"

LAWRENCE C.C. CHU Chef Chu's | Los Altos

Lawrence Chu was born in Sichuan province, China, and raised in Taiwan, Shanghai and Hong Kong. In 1970, he opened his award-winning Chef Chu's restaurant. His creative flair, firsthand knowledge of the regional cuisines of China and dedication to using the highest-quality ingredients have made Chef Chu's one of the San Francisco Bay Area's best-loved Chinese restaurants. A renowned cookbook author, lecturer and media personality, Larry recently released his newest cookbook, *Celebrating Your Place at Our Table*, commemorating his restaurant's 40th anniversary. He continually gives back to the community by supporting local charities and civic fundraisers, and is one of the founders of the Asian Culinary Association.

chefchu.com

GUEST CHEFS

SYLVAIN DELPIQUE David Burke Townhouse | New York

Sylvain Delpique grew up in Albertville, France. After graduating from Challes-les-Eaux culinary school in 2000, he relocated to the U.S. to work as chef de partie at Union League Café in New Haven, Connecticut. He moved on to Restaurant Jean-Louis in Greenwich, Connecticut, and was promoted to sous chef in just one year. Moving to New York City, he took on his native cuisine as sous chef at the French bistro Artisanal. Two years later, he found a home at David Burke Townhouse, a destination for clever and delicious modern American food. As the restaurant's executive chef, Sylvain's enthusiasm in the kitchen lends to an energetic atmosphere where creativity thrives in the form of innovative cuisine.

davidburketownhouse.com

MICHAEL GALATA Osteria del Circo | New York

Growing up in his family's New Jersey restaurant, Michael Galata discovered a talent for cooking at an early age. After graduating from high school, he took over the kitchen and helped manage the business while earning his culinary arts degree. After working for two years at New Jersey's Stage House Inn, Michael joined the staff of the Maccioni family's Le Cirque 2000, becoming sous chef there at age 22. Today he creates fabulous Italian dishes as executive chef at the Maccionis' Osteria del Circo. His passion for continually learning reflects the philosophy that "we can always grow and improve, no matter how satisfied we are with the current result."

osteriadelcirco.com

GALE GAND TRU | Chicago

Gale Gand, executive pastry chef and partner at TRU, a AAA Five Diamond restaurant recently awarded a Michelin star, was named *Pastry Chef of the Year* by the James Beard Foundation and *Bon Appétit* magazine in 2001. Gale hosted Food Network's long-running *Sweet Dreams* and has appeared on *Iron Chef America*, *Baking with Julia* and *Top Chef Just Desserts*. She is an accomplished cookbook author whose seven titles include *Chocolate and Vanilla* and *Gale Gand's Brunch!* She also has her own root beer company producing Gale's Root Beer. Gale attended culinary school at La Varenne in Paris. She is married to an environmentalist and has a 14-year-old son, Gio, and twin 6-year-old girls, Ella and Ruby.

Galegand.com

MARIA HINES Tilth | Seattle

Winner of the 2009 James Beard Foundation Award for *Best Chef: Northwest*, Maria Hines has been turning heads on the national culinary scene since she took the helm at Seattle's Earth & Ocean in 2003. In 2005, Maria was named one of *Food & Wine* magazine's 10 Best New Chefs. In 2006, she opened her own restaurant, Tilth, which features New American cuisine. In September 2006, Tilth became the second restaurant in the U.S. (after Washington, D.C.'s Restaurant Nora) to receive organic certification from the nonprofit research and education organization Oregon Tilth, and in 2008, *The New York Times* named it one of the 10 best new restaurants in the U.S.

tilthrestaurant.com

ANDY HUSBANDS   Tremont 647 & Sister Sorel | Boston
In 2010, Andy celebrated the 14th anniversary of his acclaimed restaurant Tremont 647 and the 10th anniversary of his popular café Sister Sorel. He's also currently at work on his second cookbook, *Brunch*. A master of adventurous American cuisine, the Seattle native has received local and national praise, and even showcased his talents on the hit TV show *Hell's Kitchen* in 2009. When he's not in the kitchen, Andy can be found on the competitive barbecue circuit with his team *iQUE BBQ* (sponsored by Harpoon Brewery, 2009 World Champions). He has been honored as *Chef/Restaurateur of the Year* by hunger-relief organization *Share Our Strength*, with which he has worked closely for the past 20 years.
tremont647.com

RICK MOONEN   Rick Moonen's rm seafood | Las Vegas
Rick Moonen has devoted his career to being America's top culinary advocate for sustainable seafood. A native New Yorker, he graduated first in his class from the Culinary Institute of America in Hyde Park, NY, in 1978. He apprenticed at L'Hostellerie Bressane in Hillsdale, NY, working side by side with Chef Jean Morel. In February 2005, Rick opened Rick Moonen's rm seafood at Mandalay Bay Resort & Casino. The multilevel restaurant offers regional coastal favorites, a world-class raw bar, and inventive tasting and à la carte menus. When not behind the stove, Rick can be found traveling throughout the U.S. educating about the dangers of over-fishing and the importance of ocean conservation.
rmseafood.com

BRIAN POOR   Portland City Grill | Portland, OR
Brian Poor grew up in the farmland of eastern Washington state. The sharing of meals around the family table helped inspire his interest in food. That interest took him to culinary school and then out to seek his fortune as a chef. He worked in some of Seattle's coolest restaurants, which resulted in a performance at the James Beard House in New York City. Brian also spent seven years behind the microphone with his food talk show *The Poor Man's Kitchen* on Seattle's KOMO Newsradio. Today, as director of culinary for Portland City Grill, one of the West Coast's busiest restaurants, he creates new and exciting menu items featuring local, sustainable ingredients.
portlandcitygrill.com

KENT RATHBUN   Abacus, Jasper's Restaurants, Rathbun's Blue Plate Kitchen, Zea WoodFire Grill | Texas
After rising rapidly through the ranks of some of the world's finest restaurants, Kent Rathbun continues to demonstrate his culinary skills not only with the expansion of restaurant concepts but also with his new product line, Kent Rathbun Elements. Kent has created an astounding culinary legacy in Texas and has thrived on the national scene. He has cooked at the James Beard House in New York on several occasions and has been nominated four times as the James Beard Foundation's *Best Chef: Southwest*. In 2008, Kent and his brother Kevin defeated Bobby Flay in a culinary battle on Food Network's *Iron Chef America*.
kentrathbun.com

KEVIN RATHBUN   Rathbun's, Krog Bar, Kevin Rathbun Steak | Atlanta

Kevin Rathbun is a pivotal force on the local and national restaurant scenes. In 2004, he opened Rathbun's, which features his take on Modern American cuisine and has earned accolades from *Travel & Leisure* (Best New American Restaurant) and many others. His award-winning Spanish-style wine bar, Krog Bar, opened in 2005. Kevin Rathbun Steak opened in 2007 and went on to become one of America's top steakhouses. Kevin continuously donates his time and energy to charitable events. He resides in Atlanta with his wife, Melissa, and in his spare time enjoys philanthropy, reading cookbooks, dining out, fine cigars and traveling.

rathbunsrestaurant.com

JOHN TESAR   The Tesar Restaurant Group | Dallas

Known widely for his sustainable-food ethic and seafood mastery, John is culinary director for The Tesar Restaurant Group Dallas and recently opened two new restaurants—The Commissary and The Cedars Social. He has also been responsible for the creation of three other Dallas restaurant concepts: Dallas Chop House, Dallas Fish Market and Wild Salsa. John, who was "Jimmy Sears" in Anthony Bourdain's *Kitchen Confidential*, was a semifinalist in the 2009 James Beard Foundation Awards (*Best Chef: Southwest*). During his tenure as executive chef at Rosewood Mansion on Turtle Creek, the restaurant earned rave reviews and was named one of America's best new restaurants by *Esquire*. John serves on *Share Our Strength*'s Taste of the Nation Culinary Council.

thecommissarydallas.com

WADE WIESTLING   The Oceanaire Seafood Room | Minneapolis

Wade Wiestling has been at the helm of The Oceanaire Seafood Room since 1998. Now, this award-winning recipe has created hit restaurants all over the U.S., in major cities such as Washington, D.C., Dallas, San Diego, Boston, Atlanta and Miami, just to name a few. A well-known figure on the Twin Cities restaurant scene, Wade has donated his time and talents to help many charitable events, including *Share Our Strength*'s Taste of the Nation and the *March of Dimes* Signature Chefs Auction. His guidance has led Oceanaire to five James Beard House appearances and has led 14 chefs through James Beard House kitchen events.

theoceanaire.com

JASON WILSON   Crush | Seattle

Jason Wilson, 2010 James Beard Foundation Award winner (*Best Chef: Northwest*) and alumnus of *Food & Wine* magazine's *Best New Chefs* class of 2006, is a graduate of the California Culinary Academy and has worked in kitchens as far afield as France and Singapore. In 2005, he realized a lifelong dream when he opened Crush with wife Nicole. One of Seattle's hottest restaurants and most innovative dining experiences, Crush offers seasonally changing menus that highlight the finest local, organic ingredients and sustainable seafood, as well as an award-winning wine list. The name of the restaurant was inspired by Jason and Nicole's wedding, which took place at a private estate during the 2001 crush.

chefjasonwilson.com

thank you

THIS COOKBOOK AND THE TELEVISION SERIES THAT INSPIRED IT ARE THE RESULTS OF TEAMWORK PAR EXCELLENCE.

I'd like to thank everyone who participated in the *Nick Stellino Cooking with Friends 2* project, starting with my team at KCTS/Seattle Public Television—particularly Nicole Metcalf, my television producer, and Dave Ko, my director—who helped me bring a second wonderful season of *Nick Stellino Cooking with Friends* to fruition.

My sincere appreciation also goes to Lisa Moore, my book designer, and to Tom Niemi, Don LaCombe and Jay Parikh, who have been immensely helpful to me in my endeavors. I'd also like to thank my culinary director, Bridget Charters, for her support and hard work during the taping of our shows.

As always, my wife, Nanci, was instrumental in helping me turn my vision into reality. I've said it before, and I'll say it again: Without her, none of this would exist.
I'd also like to extend my thanks to Therese Frare, who shot the photographs in this book, and to my editor, Pat Mallinson.

Finally, these acknowledgements would not be complete without a heartfelt thank-you to my family and friends for their support throughout this journey.

What started as a little, impossible dream, handwritten on a yellow pad on the kitchen table of my small apartment some 25 years ago, has become a reality beyond my wildest dreams.

I am particularly grateful to these companies that have helped us make this book and the accompanying national television series a reality:

chsugar.com

dominosugar.com

electroluxappliances.com

pompeian.com

artesawinery.com

davincipasta.com

chefrevival.com

index

A
Almond Pound Cake with Strawberries &
    Mascarpone Cream 110
Andrew's Mac & Cheese 121
Andy's First Place BBQ Glazed Pork Tenderloin
    with Bacon-Corn Relish & Cheddar Grits 93
appetizers
    Brown Sugar-Brined, Stove Top-Smoked
        Wild Salmon 132
    Brown-Sugared Pork Belly, Creamed Cabbage
        & Mustard Greens 164
    Gnudi with Arugula Pesto & Tomato 'Spuma' 54
    Grilled Honey-Glazed Quail with
        Watercress Salad 25
Applewood-Smoked Jalapeño Shrimp 145
artichokes
    Tortino of, & Calamari 47
Arugula, Romaine & Radicchio Salad with
    Glazed Pine Nuts, Prosciutto Chips &
    Gorgonzola Dressing 101
asparagus
    & Black Trumpet Mushroom Risotto with
        Truffle Foam 106
    Roasted, with Parmesan Cheese 223
    Soup with a Confit of Peppers &
        Asparagus Tips 171

B
bacon
    & Eggs with Niman Ranch Bacon &
        Duck Eggs 148
    -Corn Relish 93
    Eggnog French Toast with Blueberries &
        Brown Sugar-Crusted 61
    Smoked, -Wrapped Rabbit Loin with Wilted
        Spinach & Grapefruit Jus 41
Bacon & Eggs with Niman Ranch Bacon &
    Duck Eggs 148
Baked-Potato Salad 141
Banana Cream Pie Spoons 72
Basil-Garlic Braised Manila Clams 135
beef
    Fresh Basil, 21
    Gung Gung's Home-Style Oxtail Stew 27
    Lime & Curry-Marinated Grass-Fed Rib-Eye Steaks
        with Cucumber & Honeydew Melon Chutney
        & Spiced Basmati Rice 177
    Meatball Sandwiches 59
    Nick's Chili-Spiced Burgers 122
    Slow-Braised Short Ribs with Parsley Pistou 218
    Spaghetti & Meatballs 57
    Steak & Salad with a Balsamic-Parmesan
        Dressing 185
BLT Burrata with Chipotle-Tomato Dressing 37
Brown Sugar-Brined, Stove Top-Smoked
    Wild Salmon 132
Brown-Sugared Pork Belly, Creamed Cabbage
    & Mustard Greens 164
brunch
    Bacon & Eggs with Niman Ranch Bacon &
        Duck Eggs 148
    Cheesy Scrambled Eggs in Ham Cups 70
    Eggnog French Toast with Blueberries &
        Brown Sugar-Crusted Bacon 61
    Sea Scallop Benedict with Country Ham Grits &
        Tabasco Hollandaise 166
    Vita's Ricotta Doughnuts 63
Butternut Squash Risotto 81

C
Cajun Roasted Chicken Breasts with Shrimp
    Jambalaya Hash 143
Cannoli 49
Cauliflower & Parmesan Soup with Cured-Olive
    Crostini 161
Cauliflower Tabouleh 210
Champagne Oyster Stew 125
Cheddar Grits 93
Cheesy Scrambled Eggs in Ham Cups 70
Chef Chu's Famous Chicken Salad 29
chicken
    Cajun Roasted, Breasts with
        Shrimp Jambalaya Hash 143
    Chicharrones with Fresh Oregano 98
    Lemon-Marinated Breasts, Eggplant
        Ratatouille with 79
    Salad, Chef Chu's Famous 29
Chilled English Pea Soup with Jumbo Lump Crab 105

Chinese-Style Tea-Steamed Halibut Steaks with Scallions, Ginger & Fermented Black Beans 191
chocolate
    Chip Cookie, The Ultimate 91
    -Dipped Cake Lollipops 71
    Dried Cherry-, Fudge Cookies 151
    Easy, Mousse 187
    Meringue Tart 152
    Warm Banana-White, Crisp with Macadamia Nut Crumble 203
Chocolate Chip Cookie, The Ultimate 91
Chocolate-Dipped Cake Lollipops 71
Clams with Sausage & Tomatoes 43
coffee
    Cinnamon 65
    Orange 65
Confit of Peppers & Asparagus Tips 172
Cucumber-Melon Salad with Minted Ricotta 213

D

desserts
    Almond Pound Cake with Strawberries & Mascarpone Cream 110
    Banana Cream Pie Spoons 72
    Cannoli 49
    Chocolate-Dipped Cake Lollipops 71
    Chocolate Meringue Tart 152
    Dried Cherry-Chocolate Fudge Cookies 151
    Easy Chocolate Mousse 187
    Gooey Toffee Cakes with Toasted-Pecan Ice Cream 168
    Lemon-Lime Bars 95
    Plums Two Ways with Pound Cake 84
    Rhubarb Parfait 182
    Sticky Toffee Pudding with Butterscotch Sauce & Sour Cream Ice Cream 66
    Strawberry Sauce 75
    Tiramisù 74
    Ultimate Chocolate Chip Cookie, The 91
    Vita's Ricotta Doughnuts 63
    Warm Banana-White Chocolate Crisp with Macadamia Nut Crumble 203
Dried Cherry-Chocolate Fudge Cookies 151

E

Easy Chocolate Mousse 187
eggs
    Cheesy Scrambled, in Ham Cups 70
    Duck, Bacon & Eggs with Niman Ranch Bacon & 148
Eggnog French Toast with Blueberries & Brown Sugar-Crusted Bacon 61
Eggplant Ratatouille with Lemon-Marinated Chicken Breasts 79

F

Fat Choy Purses 15
Fig & Pepper Cress Salad with Goat's Milk Yogurt, Goat Cheese, & Meyer Lemon & Honey Vinaigrette 179
Fillet of Tomatoes Pasta 34
fish
    Brown Sugar-Brined, Stove Top-Smoked Wild Salmon 132
    Chinese-Style Tea-Steamed Halibut Steaks with Scallions, Ginger & Fermented Black Beans 191
    Fluke with Potato Gnocchi, Fava Beans & Mustard Sauce 115
    Grilled Salmon Salad with Grilled Romaine Hearts, with Blue Cheese & Bacon Vinaigrette 198
    Hot Chili Grilled Alaskan Sockeye with Fresh Summer Mango Salsa 193
    Minnesota-Style Walleye & Wild-Rice Cakes 200
    Olive Oil-Poached White Anchovies & Squid-Ink Spaghetti, Sicilian Style 175
    Pan-Roasted Wahoo with Eggplant Caviar & Local Tomato-Basil Salad 158
    Potato-Wrapped Tuna Stuffed with Crab & Cucumber, Served with Pineapple Carpaccio & Ponzu Dressing 39
    Salmon with Vodka & Lemon Sauce 205
    Salt-Crusted Branzino 48
Flavored Coffees 65
Fluke with Potato Gnocchi, Fava Beans & Mustard Sauce 115
Fresh Basil Beef 21
Fried Capers 207

G

Garlic & Lemon Grilled Shrimp with Warm Potato, Arugula & Chorizo Salad 189
Garlic & Oil Pasta 33
Garlic-Roasted Whole Dungeness Crab & Arugula-Fennel Salad 127
Gnudi with Arugula Pesto & Tomato 'Spuma' 54
Gooey Toffee Cakes with Toasted-Pecan Ice Cream 168
Grilled Honey-Glazed Quail with Watercress Salad 25
Grilled Salmon Salad with Grilled Romaine Hearts, with Blue Cheese & Bacon Vinaigrette 198
Gung Gung's Home-Style Oxtail Stew 27

H

Hot Chili Grilled Alaskan Sockeye with Fresh Summer Mango Salsa 193

K

Kabocha Bisque 18

L
Lemon-Lime Bars 95
Lime & Curry-Marinated Grass-Fed Rib-Eye Steaks
    with Cucumber & Honeydew Melon Chutney
    & Spiced Basmati Rice 177
Limed Sour Cream 99

M
Meatball Sandwiches 59
Minnesota-Style Walleye & Wild-Rice Cakes 200
mushrooms
    Asparagus & Black Trumpet, Risotto with
        Truffle Foam 106
    Veal Scaloppine alla Romana 53

N
Nick's Chili-Spiced Burgers 122
Nine-Spice Scallops 212

O
Olive Oil-Poached White Anchovies & Squid-Ink
    Spaghetti, Sicilian Style 175
Orange Blossom Ribs 23
oxtail
    Gung Gung's Home-Style, Stew 27
Ozette Potato Salad 85

P
Pan-Fried Potatoes with Peppers & Shallots 44
Pan-Roasted Wahoo with Eggplant Caviar &
    Local Tomato-Basil Salad 158
pasta
    Andrew's Mac & Cheese 121
    Fillet of Tomatoes, 34
    Garlic & Oil, 33
    Gnudi with Arugula Pesto & Tomato 'Spuma' 54
    Olive Oil-Poached White Anchovies & Squid-Ink
        Spaghetti, Sicilian Style 175
    Pork Ragù 215
    Spaghetti & Meatballs 57
    with Braised Sausages & Ricotta Parmigiana 86
peppers
    Pan-Fried Potatoes with, & Shallots 44
Plums Two Ways with Pound Cake 84
Poached Calamari Ceviche 118
pork
    Brown-Sugared, Belly, Creamed Cabbage
        & Mustard Greens 164
    Chops with Zenzero Sauce 221
    Meatball Sandwiches 59
    Orange Blossom Ribs 23
    Ragù 215
    Spaghetti & Meatballs 57
    Tenderloin, Andy's First Place BBQ Glazed 93

potato
    Baked-, Salad 141
    Gnocchi 115
    Ozette, Salad 85
    Pan-Fried, with Peppers & Shallots 44
    Warm, Arugula & Chorizo Salad, Garlic & Lemon
        Grilled Shrimp with 189
Potato-Wrapped Tuna Stuffed with Crab & Cucumber,
    Served with Pineapple Carpaccio & Ponzu
    Dressing 39

Q
quail
    Grilled Honey-Glazed, with Watercress Salad 25

R
rabbit
    Smoked Bacon-Wrapped, Loin with Wilted
        Spinach & Grapefruit Jus 41
Radicchio & Spinach Sauté with Lemon Zest & Garlic 207
Red & Gold Beet Salad 134
Rhubarb Parfait 182
Rick's New England Clam Chowder 109
ricotta
    Cannoli 49
    Doughnuts, Vita's 63
    Minted, Cucumber-Melon Salad with 213
    Parmigiana, Pasta with Braised Sausages & 86
risotto
    Asparagus & Black Trumpet Mushroom, with
        Truffle Foam 106
    Butternut Squash 81
Roasted Asparagus with Parmesan Cheese 223

S
salads
    & Shaved Parmesan, Veal Milanese with
        Tomato Pesto, 137
    Arugula-Fennel 127
    Arugula, Romaine & Raddicchio, with
        Glazed Pine Nuts, Prosciutto Chips &
        Gorgonzola Dressing 101
    Baked-Potato 141
    Chef Chu's Famous Chicken 29
    Cucumber-Melon, with Minted Ricotta 213
    Fig & Pepper Cress, with Goat's Milk Yogurt,
        Goat Cheese, & Meyer Lemon & Honey
        Vinaigrette 179
    Grilled Salmon, with Grilled Romaine Hearts,
        with Blue Cheese & Bacon Vinaigrette 198
    Ozette Potato 85
    Red & Gold Beet 134
    Steak &, with a Balsamic-Parmesan
        Dressing 185
    Tomatoes & Bread 154
    Warm Potato, Arugula & Chorizo 189
Salmon with Vodka & Lemon Sauce 205

Salsa 101 99
Salt-Crusted Branzino 48
sauces
 Butterscotch 66
 Mustard 115
 Strawberry 75
 Toffee 168
 Tomato 89
 Vodka & Lemon 205
 Zenzero 221
sausage, andouille
 Cajun Roasted Chicken Breasts with Shrimp Jambalaya Hash 143
sausage, chorizo
 Garlic & Lemon Grilled Shrimp with Warm Potato, Arugula & Chorizo Salad 189
sausage, Italian
 Clams with Sausage & Tomatoes 43
 Pasta with Braised Sausages & Ricotta Parmigiana 86
seafood
 Applewood-Smoked Jalapeño Shrimp 145
 Basil-Garlic Braised Manila Clams 135
 Brown Sugar-Brined, Stove Top-Smoked Wild Salmon 132
 Cajun Roasted Chicken Breasts with Shrimp Jambalaya Hash 143
 Champagne Oyster Stew 125
 Chilled English Pea Soup with Jumbo Lump Crab 105
 Chinese-Style Tea-Steamed Halibut Steaks with Scallions, Ginger & Fermented Black Beans 191
 Clams with Sausage & Tomatoes 43
 Fluke with Potato Gnocchi, Fava Beans & Mustard Sauce 115
 Garlic & Lemon Grilled Shrimp with Warm Potato, Arugula & Chorizo Salad 189
 Garlic-Roasted Whole Dungeness Crab & Arugula-Fennel Salad 127
 Grilled Salmon Salad with Grilled Romaine Hearts, with Blue Cheese & Bacon Vinaigrette 198
 Hot Chili Grilled Alaskan Sockeye with Fresh Summer Mango Salsa 193
 Nine-Spice Scallops 212
 Olive Oil-Poached White Anchovies & Squid-Ink Spaghetti, Sicilian Style 175
 Pan-Roasted Wahoo with Eggplant Caviar & Local Tomato-Basil Salad 158
 Poached Calamari Ceviche 118
 Potato-Wrapped Tuna Stuffed with Crab & Cucumber, Served with Pineapple Carpaccio & Ponzu Dressing 39
 Rick's New England Clam Chowder 109
 Salmon with Vodka & Lemon Sauce 205
 Salt-Crusted Branzino 48

Sea Scallop Benedict with Country Ham Grits & Tabasco Hollandaise 166
 Stove-Top Braised Octopus 209
 Tortino of Artichokes & Calamari 47
Sea Scallop Benedict with Country Ham Grits & Tabasco Hollandaise 166
sides
 Baked-Potato Salad 141
 Cauliflower Tabouleh 210
 Confit of Peppers & Asparagus Tips 172
 Fried Capers 207
 Limed Sour Cream 99
 Ozette Potato Salad 85
 Pan-Fried Potatoes with Peppers & Shallots 44
 Radicchio & Spinach Sauté with Lemon Zest & Garlic 207
 Red & Gold Beet Salad 134
 Roasted Asparagus with Parmesan Cheese 223
 Salsa 101 99
 Yams with Meringue 77
 YaYa's Eggplant Fries with Confectioners Sugar 157
Slow-Braised Short Ribs with Parsley Pistou 218
Smoked Bacon-Wrapped Rabbit Loin with Wilted Spinach & Grapefruit Jus 41
soup
 Asparagus, with a Confit of Peppers & Asparagus Tips 171
 Cauliflower & Parmesan, with Cured-Olive Crostini 161
 Champagne Oyster Stew 125
 Chilled English Pea, with Jumbo Lump Crab 105
 Kabocha Bisque 18
 Rick's New England Clam Chowder 109
Spaghetti & Meatballs 57
Steak & Salad with a Balsamic-Parmesan Dressing 185
Sticky Toffee Pudding with Butterscotch Sauce & Sour Cream Ice Cream 66
Stove-Top Braised Octopus 209
Strawberry Sauce 75

T

Tiramisù 74
tomato
 & Bread Salad 154
 BLT Burrata with Chipotle-, Dressing 37
 Clams with Sausage &, 43
 Fillet of, Pasta 34
 Pesto 137
 Salsa 101 99
 Sauce 89
 Spaghetti & Meatballs 57
 'Spuma,' Gnudi with Arugula Pesto & 54
Tortino of Artichokes & Calamari 47

U
Ultimate Chocolate Chip Cookie, The 91

V
veal
    Meatball Sandwiches 59
    Milanese with Tomato Pesto, Salad &
        Shaved Parmesan 137
    Scaloppine alla Romana 53
    Spaghetti & Meatballs 57
Vita's Ricotta Doughnuts 63

W
Warm Banana-White Chocolate Crisp with
    Macadamia Nut Crumble 203

Y
Yams with Meringue 77
YaYa's Eggplant Fries with Confectioners Sugar 157

It's all about passion!